Victorian Entertainment

The Dancing Platform at Cremorne Gardens (Phoebus Levin, 1864)
by courtesy of The London Museum

Victorian Entertainment

Alan Delgado

American Heritage Press, New York

07-016245-X

Library of Congress Catalog Card Number 74-155-881

Published by American Heritage Press,
a Subsidiary of McGraw-Hill, Inc.

Printed in Great Britain

Contents

Victorian Entertainment

One man's entertainment is another man's boredom, and much entertainment in Victorian times was simply not entertaining. Money was lavished on entertaining by those who could afford it. Servants were available in almost unlimited numbers. The leisure activities of each day culminating in dinners and dances at night were considered by some people to be of crushing boredom and monotony. Those who worked for their living in the factories and sweat shops made sure that what little money they could afford to spend on entertainment was spent to the best advantage.

The deadening afternoons when the unmarried daughters and their mother were 'at home' to any socially accepted visitors who cared to call were positively stifling. The formality of Victorian life and the strictures on behaviour made it difficult for anyone to meet anyone else without having been formally introduced. The men fared better. Away from home most of the day making money, there was the comparative informality of City life, the club to pop into before going home in the evening, and the freedom to move about unaccompanied, which women could not do.

Conversation reflected what was socially acceptable and what was not. 'Things One Would Rather Have Left Unsaid' or 'Expressed Differently' and other examples of ghastly *faux pas* were the basis for jokes in *Punch* week after week.

It was meeting the same people at the same sort of functions evening after evening which must have dampened the enthusiasm of even the most socially inclined. There may have been some who enjoyed the round of musical evenings and party games, but to the retiring, shy soul it must have been purgatory with little hope of escape. The tall, good-looking man basked in the attention of the fair sex; the small, insignificant little chap was a figure of fun. The beautiful young woman was able to select from the impeccable males surrounding her a partner for a dance, or an escort who would have the pleasure of taking her into supper. The plain frump stood awkwardly outside the magic circle until some male was practically ordered by a harrassed hostess to look after her.

The snigger behind the gloved hand or fan, the smile hidden by an opera hat against the mouth, concealed a contempt for somebody who had failed to conform to what was acceptable in looks or behaviour. Again *Punch*, which mirrored society life, reflected this attitude in the jokes and cartoons which appeared from its inception until Queen Victoria's death and after.

What really entertained, it seems, were the social gaffes made by those who, for physical or emotional reasons, could not or would not conform in a way that was considered 'normal'. The intellectual was suspect; the eccentric was a joke who was good for a well-bred laugh.

The sharp social divisions that existed were also sources of entertainment. The wealthy were patronisingly amused by the antics of the poor, and the poor found the habits of the wealthy equally amusing although they could not afford to be patronising about them.

Outside the home, entertainment abounded. In the streets, the taverns, the music halls, the pleasure gardens—it was all boisterous, vulgar, uninhibited and genuinely entertaining. In the early part of the Queen's reign entertainment was to be found in the neighbourhood, but the coming of the railways and other methods of transport changed people's way of life, the work they did and how they lived. Increased mobility enabled them to go further afield for their amusements.

By the 1850s and 60s the working classes had intruded on the privacy of the wealthy. Delightful resorts and beauty spots known only to the upper classes were invaded by hordes of uncouth people who needed accommodation, food and entertainment. Thank goodness, then, for the Continent. The Channel between Brighton and Boulogne was a natural hazard not many of the working class were willing to face, although Cook's tours introduced the delights of continental travel to an increasing number of people towards the end of the century.

ANNALS OF A RETIRED SUBURB.

Mrs. Boultby Smith and her Daughters have been "at Home" to their London Friends every Wednesday Afternoon for the last Seven Years. Last Wednesday some Visitors actually came!

1882

Worse still, women were no longer content to be left at home. They were becoming more athletic and wished to take part in sporting activities which had hitherto been masculine preserves.

The tendency to make entertainment 'respectable' was evident during the course of the Queen's long reign. Reforms were necessary. The blatant abuses of the racing community were largely eliminated by the increased area of influence of the Jockey Club; the hooliganism which at times resulted in injury to people and damage to property when a football was kicked around, was brought under control when the Football Association was established. The brutality of prize-fighting was a public scandal, and so were public hangings. The increase in population made it essential that standards in safety and hygiene should be enforced. Eating and drinking when watching a music hall performance was an accepted form of entertainment, but by the end of the century the chairs and tables had been replaced by rows of upholstered, fixed seats in the interest of safety and cleanliness. Eating and drinking had to be enjoyed elsewhere.

It was all much less fun. Although the Victorians were spared the doubtful blessings of an entertainment industry, commercial interests realised there was money to be made. The regulations, however necessary they may have been, could not be complied with unless places of entertainment were re-built. The clutches of Moss and Stoll on the music halls converted the shabby, familiar buildings into palaces of variety. There was no turning back.

The new gas lighting and the deep pile carpets, the flunkeys and the footmen, the theatres newly decorated and upholstered, the more comfortable seating—all this attracted the wealthy who had hitherto been repelled by the discomfort, the behaviour of audiences and the smell of oranges. Shirt-fronts and sables adorned the stalls; cloth caps and chokers filled the pit.

The stage was set for the Edwardians.

At Home

Casual entertainment in the homes of the wealthy was not to be tolerated. Everything had to be done on the grandest scale that a family could afford. The dining and drawing rooms of Victorian houses, so cluttered with furniture that it was difficult to move without knocking over an occasional table, were the setting for the guests who arrived by carriage resplendently dressed.

Some of the guests might bring their own servants to wait at table if the hostess for any reason was short of staff, but for normal entertaining there were generally sufficient parlourmaids, housemaids or menservants to cope with the situation. Dinner parties for a dozen or more were quite usual and the hostess spent much of her time making the arrangements.

The amount of cutlery, dishes and table linen in a Victorian household was prodigious: silver or silver-plated soup tureens, huge dishes to contain joints or fish; knives, spoons and forks of different sizes; glass of various colours and shapes for a variety of wines, and table-napkins folded in complicated shapes. Accessories such as finger bowls filled with water (sometimes warm) in which guests dipped their fingers after eating fruit, a silver utensil filled with hot water in which the gravy ladle was dipped and suitably warmed—all this was laid on a double-damask table cloth, and the sight of the sparkling silver and glass was rewarding and impressive. What organisation must have been necessary to achieve so much!

1883

THINGS ONE WOULD RATHER HAVE LEFT UNSAID.

Hostess. "WHAT FUN YOU SEEM TO BE HAVING OVER THERE, CAPTAIN SMILEY! I WISH YOU ALL SAT AT THIS END OF THE TABLE!"

A musical evening, 1879

Before dinner the guests assembled in the drawing room. There they were paired off—a gentleman being notified which lady he was to take into dinner. When the announcement 'dinner is served' was made by a servant, the gentleman would take the lady's arm and escort her to the dining room. At each place at the table a hand-written card was laid bearing the name of the guest who was to sit there. The seating of the guests was a matter of considerable concern to the hostess. There was much discussion beforehand as to the correct blending of temperaments. Guests were diverse creatures. The shy had to be drawn out—not terrified so that they became even more withdrawn; the talkative must be subdued. The placing of the guests was not an easy task for the host and hostess. A mistake in the seating arrangements could ruin an evening. It was their duty to set the conversational pace and it was the duty of the gentleman guests to see that the ladies whom they had taken into dinner were enjoying themselves. Ideally the conversation should flow easily, the laughter be discreet and the serving of the numerous courses impeccable.

At the sideboard the servants stood stiffly as the guests entered the dining room. As soon as the guests were seated they moved swiftly and silently. They knew their duties. Plates were removed and others put in their place, glasses were filled and refilled and the dishes handed round.

In 1863 Mrs Beeton suggested this menu for a dinner of twelve persons:

First course

Soupe à la Reine. Julienne Soup. Turbot and Lobster Sauce. Slices of Salmon à la Genevese. *Entrées*: Croquettes of Leveret. Fricandeau de Veau. Vol-au-Vent. Stewed Mushrooms.

Second course

Forequarter of Lamb. Guinea Fowls. Charlotte à la Parisienne. Orange Jelly. Meringues. Ratafia Ice Pudding. Lobster Salad. Sea Kale.

Desert and Ices.

This was of modest proportions compared with what was consumed at dinner parties in the 1830s.

1882

A GALLANT REPLY.

Miss Lucy. "HERE'S WHERE YOU AND I ARE TO SIT, MAJOR!"
The Major. "BY JOVE!—A—RATHER A WARM PLACE!"

Miss Lucy. "WHAT—YOU A MAJOR, AND CAN'T STAND FIRE!"
The Major. "NOT AT MY BACK, YOU KNOW, MISS LUCY!"

'The Health of the Bride', 1889

After dinner the ladies left the dining room and the men remained with their coffee and port, to talk about matters of purely masculine interest. The ladies, in the meantime, having had an opportunity to see to their faces, sipped coffee in the drawing room, and gossiped about matters of mutual interest to them. At last, in the dining room, the cry went up, 'Shall we join the ladies?' and with a certain amount of reluctance the gentlemen staggered to their feet (more often than not unsteadily) and made their uncertain way to the drawing room.

In the 1840s it was not unusual for a gentleman to be so intoxicated that he was not in a fit condition to join the ladies. In that event his servant would come to his aid, call his carriage, take him home and put him to bed. Some hours later his wife, home from the party, would join him in the bedroom. The Queen disliked this excessive drinking and insisted in court circles that the men should not be left to themselves for too long after dinner.

There were other ways of showing hospitality but all offered opportunities for eating and drinking. Balls and supper balls were staged in even more impressive surroundings. Rooms were banked with flowers and in Mrs Beeton's view the appetites of sixty dancers could not be satisfied unless there were at least sixty-two dishes and appropriate wines for consumption.

The orchestra played the popular waltzes of the day and the couples assembled on the dance floor for the quadrille. 'Lead the lady through the quadrille,' advises a book on etiquette. 'Do not *drag* her, nor clasp her hand as if it were made of wood, lest she not unjustly think you a boor.' The polka, in the forties, caused something of a sensation when it was introduced.

Less elaborate forms of entertainment included the Soirée. Cards were played and other games such as Commerce, Speculation and Limited Loo. Counters were used instead of money until the last round when the players settled their debts in cash.

Charades, dumb crambo and similar games 'broke the ice' although the shy and withdrawn must have suffered agonies by having to make themselves conspicuous. There was always a piano—more likely than not of German origin—and a song from a young lady or gentleman in the party was a welcome interlude in an evening's activities. Refreshments were served in the drawing room between half-past eight and nine o'clock. While the young people were enjoying themselves, the parents and their friends might be in another room playing cards.

Blind Man's Buff

Shadow Buff

Apart from card games there were 'Games of Action'—Blind Man's Buff, Hunt the Slipper, Twirl the Teacher or My Lady's Toilet, etc; 'Games with Pen and Pencil, or Involving Mental Exertion'—Consequences, the 'Twenty Questions', What is my Thought Like?, etc; 'Catch Games'—The Cook Who Doesn't Like Peas, He can Do Little who can't do This, etc; 'Forfeits'—To Put One Hand where the other cannot Touch It, To Kiss the Lady you Love Best without Any One Knowing It, etc.

More complicated were amateur theatricals involving the construction of stages, the taking of doors off hinges and the hope that 'paterfamilias' will be reasonable about it all. Shadow Pantomime with the screen of muslin (for preference) tightly stretched on a wooden frame, and the complex arrangements for 'Tableaux Vivants' and 'The (Living) Waxwork Exhibition' meant considerable preparation.

Magic with coins and cards ('The Four Kings being placed under the Hand of one Person and the Four Sevens under the Hand of Another, to make them Change Places at Command'), and magic with miscellaneous props enabling, for example, the performer 'to indicate on the Dial of a Watch the Hour Secretly Thought Of', passed the time pleasantly enough.

Finally there were 'After Dinner Accomplishments' consisting of more or less eccentric forms of amusement which 'when conversation chances to flag over the walnuts and wine' or over the afternoon cup of tea in the drawing room 'may be employed to advantage'. Such accomplishments involved constructing a tortoise from muscatel raisins and their stalks, or making a pig from a lemon. If it could be managed, perhaps the conversation might be channelled into the fascinating subject of spiritualism when it could be demonstrated that it was possible to elongate and/or compress the human frame.

The first essential was to select a good leader, 'who may be either a gentleman or a lady, as circumstances will admit. The principal qualification is a knowledge of the game. . . . If the person selected possesses, in addition, a commanding presence, ready wit, brilliant imagination, and quick invention, so much the better. If not, he or she will probably get on very well without them.'

The Feather Game

To be 'the life and soul of the party' was a useful social asset. Always to be in demand for parties meant never a dull moment—or did it? The endless social round, meeting the same people evening after evening, eating similar food, playing the same games—there were those who found it tedious—especially women like Florence Nightingale and Elizabeth Garrett Anderson who felt that life had more to offer, and broke away from the social circle in which they felt trapped, to do something useful with their time.

When not entertaining, but left to their own resources, the Victorian family settled down after dinner to an evening of gentle entertainment. Father might read out loud to his wife and daughters while they engaged in cross-stitch. The production of rugs, chair seats, embroidered covers and the like was impressive. So much of the work was meticulous and beautiful; so much of it was not. The painted fire-screens, the fruit and flowers lovingly modelled in wax (although we have no cause to smile in this plastic age of the twentieth century), the colourful cushions, the decorated bell-pulls—all that was to clutter still more the rooms of the Victorian upper and middle classes. The women worked diligently at pressing flowers in beautifully tooled albums, and arranging with loving care the shells and other treasures gathered from the beach during a happy summer holiday. These activities whiled away the long hours from after dinner to bedtime.

Musical Fright

Crying Forfeits

There were also books, but only the wealthy could afford to buy the three-decker novels at 31s 6d. In 1842, Charles Mudie opened his library where subscribers, paying a guinea a year, could borrow books that hitherto they had been compelled to buy. It was necessary for Mr Mudie to be a realist. Books of questionable taste were not to be allowed on the shelves. The test was simple enough : 'Would you or would you not give that book to your daughter of sixteen to read?' Consequently—to name two books—Meredith's *The Ordeal of Richard Feverel* and *The Morals of Mayfair* by Mrs Anne Edwardes were, according to the moral and social climate of the day, 'not available'.

Later, W. H. Smith developed the circulating library through their provincial shops, and by the nineties novels were being published in single volumes. Books considered unsuitable in the early part of the Queen's reign became 'acceptable' and new books were appearing that could only be described as 'shockers', but these were demanded from the libraries and the demand was met.

B

The Entertaining Streets

The urchin or time-wasting delivery boy was a common enough sight in Victorian days. There was so much taking place in the streets that was entertaining. The wealthy, beautifully dressed couple descending the steps of their house to enter a carriage was a scene to be stared at wide-eyed, and perhaps it was possible to earn a penny for opening the carriage door. The family going on holiday, the stacked luggage seen through the open front door, the horse-drawn brake by the kerbside preparatory to loading, while in the hall the servants line up to wish their master and mistress farewell. The children stand on the front steps excited but restrained. The curtains at the windows are drawn, the blinds lowered and, unseen from the street, the dust sheets cover the furniture.

To the poorly clad boy standing on the pavement at a safe distance it was all entertainment—a kind of fairyland world into which he was unlikely to enter. When the entertainment was over he would jerk his mind back to reality and run along the pavement, conscious of having wasted his employer's valuable time. There was always something else to watch and enjoy in the next street.

The street traders—the ice cream men, the balloon lady, the shoe black, the sellers from barrows of clothes, glass, china and bric-a-brac—were suitable subjects for an urchin's taunts. Giving sauce and

1897

THE ENTERPRISING TEUTON. (A Sketch in a London Suburb.)

THE CLOSE OF THE SEASON.

Housemaid (to Constant Visitor). "MISSIS SENDS YOU THIS, AND YOU NEEDN'T COME AGAIN, FOR WE'RE ALL GOING TO THE SEA-SIDE ON SATURDAY."

Mendicant. "TELL THE LADY I'M MUCH OBLIGED TO HER, AND I'M GOING TO THE SEA-SIDE MYSELF NEXT WEEK!"

1872

skipping away before an aimed blow found its target was as enjoyable as it was exciting. Imitating a doddering old gentleman walking down the street, or copying the gestures of an eccentric old lady was good sport. These cheeky talents of the working class were *so* amusing to the upper class as many jokes in *Punch* of that period confirmed. All this type of entertainment could be enjoyed free, but there were occasions when payment was expected.

The German band and the Italian hurdy-gurdy, or the barrel organ with the monkey perched on top dressed in military uniform with a miniature rifle or sword which it manipulated at its master's command—any of these could be expected at a street corner. Passers-by dropped coins into hats or hands; children at nursery windows (barred for safety) with nanny standing stiff and starched in the background, would throw down pennies on to the road. The music would stop suddenly in the middle of a tune while the performer picked up the money. Some of the coins rolled into the gutter or might have landed in a basement area. Then the children would shout and point to where the coins were hidden. Darting from one side of the road to the other the musician would gather up the money and look up at the window with a broad grin, doff a hat, perhaps, and return to the barrel organ which would resume the tune. The children would leave the window for the security of the nursery, and if it was late in the evening, nanny would draw the curtains.

RUDE INQUIRY.

Street Arabs. " HOO CURLS YER 'AIR, GOV'NOUR ? "

1864

20

THE ULSTER.

Schoolboy (to Brown, in his new great-coat). "YAH! COME OUT OF IT! D'YOU THINK I DON'T SEE YER!!"

1875

THE DRAWING ROOM.

(A STOPPAGE OF A FEW MINUTES IS SUPPOSED TO TAKE PLACE.)

Dreadful Boy (on Lamp Post). "OH! MY EYE, BILL! 'ERE 'S A ROSE BUD!"

1863

The buskers, the Punch-and-Judy men, the street musicians—all those who eked out a precarious living by entertaining the public—made their way from the crowded town centres to the residential districts. In the wide streets, free from traffic, there would be singing or music and from a house a servant might come with a coin, telling the musicians that they must go away because the lady of the house is 'resting' or the master is 'sick and must not be disturbed'. Occasionally there would be a welcome and a shower of money would be theirs to pick up. The chill winds that blew down the empty streets in the late afternoon on a winter's day accentuated the security and comfort within the tall houses on either side, and the red glow from the curtained windows was eventually extinguished by the closed shutters or drawn blinds.

Photographers frequented the parks and open spaces and did a brisk business with the nannies and the nursemaids. Photographs of their young charges were shown to delighted parents who requested more photographs to be taken. Sundays and Good Friday were the most profitable days when as much as 36 shillings might be taken. When there was an important race meeting the photographers took up their stand near the course. Celebrated owners delighted in being snapped. The Duke of Beaufort paid £1 for a photograph and 10 shillings for a second. The Prince of Wales also paid £1—his sovereign price, as he liked to call it—but any photographer who tried to take more was moved on by the police.

Donkey rides were popular. The animals were purchased each season, and females were favoured because they gave a less jolting ride. As they were often in foal at the end of the season they could be sold for more than was paid for them. It cost 1s 6d a day to keep a donkey. Ladies were sometimes prepared to pay 5s or 6s a day for the exclusive use of a particular donkey for their children to ride, and at least one lady undertook to pay 4s a day during the winter months so that her child's favourite donkey should not be sold at the end of the season.

In Manchester a group of entertainers walked about on stilts and peered into the upper floor windows of houses, much to the bewilderment of the occupants who wondered where on earth they had appeared from. There was the acrobat and conjuror whose cup-and-ball trick attracted a wide audience. After the usual preliminaries which initially drew the crowd around him, he would throw up into the air a heavy iron ball which he would catch in a metal cup placed firmly in the nape of his neck. His back being turned away from the ball, the great thrill was—would the ball miss the cup and strike him on the head? It never did, but the exciting doubt remained.

A remunerative source of income for those with debts to settle was to take an active part in the Fifth of November processions. Giant effigies arrayed in spangles and paper were paraded in the streets and it was customary for the men and boys taking part to dress up as clowns to amuse the public. The effigies were not necessarily of Guy Fawkes. Figures in the public eye who had gained some notoriety

1886

"THOSE YELLOW SANDS!"
The Browns depart for the Sea-side, to the wistful admiration of their less fortunate Neighbours.

Italian street musicians, c 1877

Smile, please! c 1877

24

November effigies, c 1877

Who's next? c 1877

The Windmill Man, c 1880

'Jack-in-the-Green', 1893

Lemonade! c 1890

were fair game or, as during the Crimean War, the enemy in the shape of Tsar Nicholas was a topical target at which to jeer.

It was mostly in the poorer districts that the parades took place. The occasional rowdyism that followed in their wake was distasteful to those living in the smarter neighbourhoods. The careworn men leading the procession, thankful for the money they received, might collect as much as 30 shillings on the 5th, £1 on the 6th and 10 or 15 shillings on the 7th. The cost of setting up the effigies had to be taken out of that, and there were a number of others who were entitled to a share. The effigies were not burnt. The clothes and spangles were carefully preserved and used the following years. All that went up in flames were the wood shavings.

In London's streets there was pageantry. A clerk or a man in a small way of business could, with his family, feel part of the social scene. Dressed in their best and mingling with the crowds there were the bright colourful uniforms at St James's to see, the playing of the quadrille by military bands in Kensington Gardens to listen to, the riders in Rotten Row to admire. If one had any kind of position in life, however humble, there was a feeling of taking part in the 'season'. To be on the fringe of a crowd was all that was necessary. Savouring the sights, cheering the soldiers and the Queen, becoming involved, however remotely, was everybody's democratic right. The glittering social scene was there for all to enjoy at a respectful distance.

27

Street scene, Lambeth, c 1890

The Pleasure Gardens

The streets led to the pleasure gardens which began to decline in the early years of Queen Victoria's reign. Vauxhall Gardens, famous since its opening in about 1661, was closed in 1840 but reopened in July 1841. Two years later it was bought at an auction for £20,000. Between 1842 and 1859 there were galas and masquerades; gas lamps replaced oil but traditions were already fading when the musicians of the orchestra no longer wore their familiar cocked hats. A Grand Venetian Carnival lit by 60,000 lamps took place in 1849, but four years later the gardens were frequented by disreputable characters who disturbed the peace of the inhabitants near by. There were complaints, and the builders took possession. On the 12 acres, once the scene of every form of eighteenth-century entertainment, houses appeared, as well as the church of St Peter, Vauxhall, to rally the faithful.

Vauxhall Gardens were replaced by Cremorne Gardens originally part of Lord Cremorne's estate set in delightful surroundings between the Thames and the King's Road, Chelsea. When it was purchased in 1830 it was converted first into a sports arena and later, in 1846, into a pleasure garden.

As a pleasure garden it was a fairyland. The lighting was brilliant but not obtrusive because the trees that surrounded the gardens cast shadows across the paths and lawns. Music filled the air; the flowers

Cremorne at the height of the season, c 1858

Derby Night at Cremorne, 1871. Picking a filly for the Oaks?

CREMORNE
GARDENS.

Open on WHIT-MONDAY, May 31, 1852.

A GRAND GALA & BALLOON ASCENT

By the celebrated Spanish Aeronaut, GUISEPPE LUNARDINI,
who will make his First Appearance this Season.

M. EUGENE ROCHEZ AND HIS COMICAL DOGS.

PERFORMANCES ON THE TIGHT ROPE

By MDLLE. VIOLANTE.

PROFESSOR TAYLOR & HIS SON, THE DOUBLE-SIGHTED YOUTH.

Grand Vocal and Instrumental Concert
BY THE CREMORNE BAND.

Conducted by BOSISIO.

THE NEW GRAND BALLET

Entitled AZURINE, or the Naiad of the Enchanted Waters.

CREMORNE BRASS BAND,

Led by SIDNEY DAVIS, will Play Selections during the Afternoon.

BRANDON LEDGER'S TROUPE OF ETHIOPIAN HARMONISTS.

CLASSICAL ILLUSTRATIONS OF SCULPTURE AND DESIGN.

DANCING TO ALL THE NEW AND FASHIONABLE MUSIC.

Kaffir Chiefs from their Native Wilds.

TERRIFIC ASCENT BY MDLLE. VIOLANTE,

SURROUNDED BY A

MAGNIFICENT DISPLAY OF FIREWORKS

BY THE CHEVALIER MORTRAM.

Doors open at Three o'clock. Balloon Ascent at Half-past Seven.

Admission, ONE SHILLING. Children, Half-Price.

SUNDAYS, after Four o'Clock——ADMISSION FREE, by Refreshment Card, SIXPENCE.

PETTER, DUFF, AND CO. PLAYHOUSE YARD, BLACKFRIARS.

Battersea to Cremorne the hard way. The year is 1861 and the female Blodin nearly
came to grief when she was half way across.

were a delight. In the summer, weather permitting, a slow steamer filled with visitors who had paid 3d
for the fare, left the City for the Cremorne Pier. Entrance to the gardens was 1 shilling and the
moment the visitor was through the gates the evening's entertainment began. Prominent, and lit with
a brilliance that was breathtaking, stood the pagoda surrounded by a dance floor which could, it was
anticipated, accommodate 4,000 people. There was a band of fifty, belting out the popular tunes of the
day. A master of ceremonies, in fine voice, made appropriate announcements but it was all quite in-
formal. The visitors consisted of clerks, shop assistants, medical students, and young men, fashionably
dressed, from Oxford and Cambridge, all accompanied by their young women. The man-about-town,
knowing what was what, rubbed shoulders with the bewildered country cousin ignorant of London's
wicked ways and a prey for the unscrupulous. The 'flash' fellows threaded their way from group to
group, sorting out the innocents who might be of benefit to them. It was not a place for the unaccompanied woman. If she was alone there was only one interpretation to be placed upon her presence.

As the evening progressed so did the pace. At half-past eight dancing began quietly enough. Later
there were fireworks and other attractions and the crowds moved away from the dance floor. Their
place was taken by a wealthier set, appropriately partnered, who found the comparative emptiness of
the dance floor more to their liking. By eleven o'clock, or later, the gardens had become uncomfortably full. The noise from the sideshows punctuated by the short, sharp 'phut' from the shooting range,
and the shouting of stall holders, transformed a peaceful garden into a bedlam. Even so, the gardens

were large enough for the romantically inclined to sit and cuddle, or just watch the scene that passed before them. Refreshment bars were scattered throughout the grounds, but those in the know, and with the money, went to Cremorne House for a splendid half-crown supper, its enjoyment enhanced by a discreet glass of Cremorne Sherry—'free from acidity and highly recommended to invalids'. In 1848 the American influence was noticed by the addition of an American Bowling Green and appropriate transatlantic drinks to suit the occasion.

West of the gardens was a circus which came from Astleys. A theatre had been built in the south, and north of the long lawn was a smaller theatre with a very popular puppet show. A maze elsewhere in the gardens enabled loving couples to become hopelessly and happily lost.

All this was pleasant and enjoyable enough, but more was needed to hold the crowds. Their attention was diverted by spectaculars, masquerades and a series of ever-changing entertainments which compelled the people to visit the gardens night after night to see what was new.

Batty's Grand National Hippodrome, Kensington, in the year of the Great Exhibition. The audience was under cover; the arena was in the open. Tournaments, chariot races, Trojan youths, and Thessalian steeds 'on a scale of extent and grandeur hitherto unattempted in England'. Also in the programme were two ostriches of the desert with their Arab riders, one of whom was thrown. And for good measure a monkey riding and driving four ponies.

C

In 1851 the Aquatic Tournament or Naval Fête was set on the river esplanade. A fortress had been erected and at 11 o'clock at night it was 'attacked' by some fourteen steamers of the Citizen Company. Accompanying the 'fleet' was the hull of an ancient steamer filled with explosive material. In order to ward off the impending 'attack' a cascade of 'fire' and smoke enveloped the 'fleet'. The excited cries of the spectators mingled with the noise and confusion, but the climax was reached when the derelict hull burst into flames, the structure blown into the air. Burning pieces of the hull hit the water with a hiss.

In 1858 the Italian Salamander whose name was Cristoforo Buona Core, entered a fiery furnace and emerged unscathed. His performance was no doubt inspired by the activities of the fire-eater Chabert who, in 1826, at White Conduit House, had entered a huge oven supported by four pillars. Before his act he is alleged to have consumed arsenic, oxalic acid, boiling oil and molten lead, and once in the oven cooked a leg of lamb and rump steak which he carved and distributed to the spectators.

Balloon ascents were very popular. In August 1852 an intrepid M Bouthellier forsook the comparative safety of the car attached to the balloon, and suspended himself from a trapeze attached to the car. When the balloon was sufficiently high he twisted and turned until the more squeamish spectators covered their eyes because they could not bear to look any longer. Braver souls then saw him suspended by the neck and later the heels.

Not to be outdone, Madame Poitevin, dressed as Europa, sat on a heifer attached to a balloon. Slowly airborne, with gracious gestures, Madame Poitevin was in for a nasty shock when she and the heifer landed. There were protests, and she was fined for cruelty to animals. This indignity must have been all the more hurtful because in Paris she and her husband had been airborne sitting on a bull and a horse and nobody had objected. In England such matters were treated differently, although a balloonist mounted on a pony had been airborne without any complaints resulting.

The more adventurous and daring balloon ascents were, the more the spectators acclaimed the performers, but there was a degree of chance. A sudden gust of wind, a failure to rise high enough or a tendency to come down in the wrong place were risks that were taken with little regard to safety.

About seven o'clock one summer evening in 1854, the fifty-year-old Henri Latour lashed himself to a parachute shaped like a horse which was suspended from a balloon. Something went wrong and the balloon landed in the Tottenham Marshes dragging Latour over the ground and through trees until he died from his terrible injuries.

A similar fate met de Groof the flying man. He constructed a 12ft stand suspended some 30ft from the balloon. From this stand he manipulated monster wings some 37ft long, and a tail 18ft long. At the first attempt he landed safely at Brandon in Essex, but in July 1874, when he repeated the experiment, it ended in disaster.

On the last occasion the balloon rose to a great height and for a horrifying half-hour hovered over the gardens. Then, with dramatic suddenness the wind changed and the balloon with de Groof in the stand was blown towards St Luke's Church, Chelsea. The man in the car of the balloon called out in German (de Groof speaking no English) 'I must cut you loose'. De Groof indicated that such action was acceptable and that he would land in the churchyard. Suddenly the stand was seen to collapse and fall like a stone into what is now Sydney Street. De Groof died from his injuries, and the balloon with its occupant came down on the Great Eastern Railway line near Springfield in Essex, narrowly missing a train. It was a sensational tragedy and a broadsheet was published at the time which included these words:

> Your feeling hearts, list to my story,
> It is a most heartrending tale;
> And when the facts are laid before you
> To drop a tear you cannot fail.

The spectacle at Cremorne that failed. De Groof plunges to his death in July 1874

'Curiosities' at the Surrey Gardens. The two native attendants 'belong to tribes that hardly ever wander away from their homes on the shores of the White Nile. . . . They appear much attached to their charge, addressing the giraffes affectionately by their Arabic names. . . .'

The air had its fascination. It was uncharted territory, so when in 1869 a French 'captive' balloon of linen and rubber securely tethered to the ground was available to passengers there were plenty of people who wanted to go. The car attached to it held thirty passengers. An engine supplied the power that let out the rope gradually until the balloon soared high over London. What an experience! The fare was 10 shillings but there was no charge for a woman inmate of the Fulham Workhouse who celebrated her hundredth birthday by taking the trip. The matron of the workhouse accompanied her.

Tight-rope walking was also an attraction although Madame Genviève nearly met with disaster when she attempted to cross the Thames on a rope. It was August 1861. Born Selina Young, she took the more romantic name of Genviève, and when she began her journey on the rope which was suspended nearly 100ft above the river, the crowds thronged the gardens and Embankment. Madame Genviève made cautious progress, but after forty-five minutes she stopped. The crowd gasped. Some-

Tortoise, upwards of 200 years old, from India at the Surrey Zoological Gardens, 1852

The balloon—

thing was wrong. Perilously the rope swayed from side to side. Surely she must fall? Boats rushed to her aid. Cords, which she grabbed, were thrown over the rope, and with difficulty she managed to lower herself into a boat—and safety. It transpired that the guy ropes had been cut by some villain who had stolen the lead weights that held them. The following year when she was performing at Highbury she slipped on a damp tight-rope and fell, crippling herself for life.

In addition to the more conventional forms of entertainment there were the unconventional. Natator, the man-frog, twenty years old, could be viewed through the glass front of a large water-tank in which he swam about imitating the movements of underwater creatures.

There were tournaments between jousting knights—appropriately dressed—which *The Illustrated London News* found tedious as they went on so long. An evening in 1858 was to be devoted to an 'Aristocratic Fête'. A committee of ladies and gentlemen whose social standing was in accordance with the title of the fête, organised the event and sold tickets. A difficulty confronting the ladies of the committee was the request from the gentlemen of the committee for tickets to give to the not-so-aristocratic ladies they wished to invite. Fortunately their embarrassment was washed away by a heavy fall of rain and the fête did not take place.

Fireworks, bonfires, smoke and bangs—that is what the people liked. Famous land and sea battles, portrayed in action, were best suited for this, and at a time when patriotic fervour was at its height the cheers resounded.

On a quieter note there was farce, vaudeville and ballet at the theatre, while in the grounds a certain Herr Von Joel, an elderly German gentleman, would appear unexpectedly in various parts of the gardens and give an imitation of birds singing. Another of his accomplishments was yodelling in the Swiss manner.

Unfortunately, despite all these varied attractions that gave so much pleasure, the gardens became more and more rowdy. There was vandalism. Pavilions were damaged, bars were wrecked and the police were compelled to restore law and order. The noise became intolerable and residents living nearby were unable to sleep at nights. There was always the danger of the rowdy elements harming the public. From 1870 the situation worsened, and in 1877 Cremorne Gardens were finally closed.

The site of Batty's Hippodrome is now occupied by most of De Vere Gardens. Its situation when it opened in May 1851, nearly opposite the Broad Walk in Kensington Gardens between Victoria Road and the present Palace Gate, was a pleasant one and the crowds flocked to see what Walter Batty, the circus proprietor, had to offer. The stirring sound of two brass bands drew the spectators to the Hippodrome where, for as little as sixpence, they were admitted. There they thrilled to the skills of the Debach Brothers each controlling six horses, the hooves thundering round the arena. This exciting chariot race was followed by the breathtaking Barbary Race between twelve horses without riders. Outside, the more familiar balloon ascents took place. Despite the showmanship and excitement the Hippodrome closed after a year and during the 1860s was used as a riding school.

At the same time as Batty opened the Hippodrome, Alexis Soyer, chef at the Reform Club and later to become culinary adviser to Florence Nightingale in the Crimea, established what was known as Soyer's Symposium, Kensington. Details of it were printed on satin paper with green-tinted edges. A single ticket cost one guinea; a 'family' ticket three guineas irrespective, it appears, of the size of the family.

The house Soyer had acquired for his enterprise was Gore House belonging to Lady Blessington. He transformed it into different restaurants specialising in exotic dishes so that there was variety for the

—goes up
Poplar Recreation Ground, c 1892

most jaded palate. Each room was appropriately named. There was the Blessington Temple of the Muses; the Salle de Noces de Danae; the Roscaille of Eternal Snow; the Bower of Ariadne (depicting vineyards against an Italian landscape); the Celestial Hall of Golden Lilies (for those who liked Chinese dishes) to mention a few. The garden was a beautiful setting and in the 'park' (renamed Pré d'Orsay) which Soyer rented from a man who grazed cows in it, was a dining hall some 400ft long with a table over 300ft in length and a tablecloth to cover it.

An average of a thousand people a day visited the Symposium, but it closed suddenly five months after it had opened. Such a vast undertaking required better management than it was getting and, more important, the food when it was served failed to live up to the exotic-sounding names of the different restaurants in which it was consumed.

The Surrey Zoological Gardens (season tickets a guinea; 1 shilling at the gate) situated between the Kennington and Walworth Roads rivalled the zoo at Regent's Park. In 1836 it housed giraffes from Alexandria—the first ever to be seen in England. Other exhibits included an orang-outang, an Indian one-horned rhinoceros and an £800 lion named Nero. In the grounds small children had rides on the giant tortoises. Even the balloon ascents sometimes had a zoological flavour. Mr and Mrs Graham owned a monkey named Signor Jacopo which they dressed in a scarlet coat and feathers. The monkey, lifted in the balloon, was released by parachute on to Walworth Common and the fortunate person who found the animal and returned it to the Grahams was rewarded with the grand sum of £2.

In 1838 the attempted ascent of the Montgolfier balloon nearly caused a riot. It was more of a structure than a balloon. It was as high as the York Column with a circumference nearly half that of the dome of St Paul's. Its inflation was complicated by the use of chopped straw burnt in a brazier under the bag of the balloon. When, for the second time, the balloon caught fire, the ascent was abandoned. Rowdier elements in the crowd of 5,000 spectators attempted to seize the official responsible and duck him in a pond, but they were unsuccessful. Instead the balloon was stoned. The glass conservatory in which the lions were kept was also shattered but the trouble-makers were diverted by the eruption of Vesuvius—a set-piece panorama motivated by fireworks in a spectacular and deafening manner—and then by the arrival of the police.

Panoramas were a great attraction. As well as Vesuvius in eruption, there was the burning of Old London in 1666, the Siege of Gibraltar, the Storming of Badajoz and the Taking of Sebastopol. The background settings were skilfully painted. Any event that was both patriotic and stirring, and involved the exploding of fireworks, the smell of smoke and the sight of fire was the kind of spectacle that people came to see.

In 1855 the animals were sold and a music hall erected on the site to hold an audience of 12,000 and an immense orchestra. For six years it flourished. All the great stars of variety appeared there. When a fire burnt the music hall to the ground a theatre was built in its place and the gardens offered similar entertainment to that at Cremorne. Comi opera and ballet, orchestral concerts and bands, dancing and spectaculars entertained those who came. In 1878 it closed, but not before a boxing match took place between Rooke and Harrington for a magnificent silver vase worth £100. An uncouth crowd of some 800 came to watch the match and see the vase proudly displayed. A waiter, remembering the old zoological days, recognised the 'silver' vase for what it really was—namely a drinking vessel made of lead which had stood on one of the counters.

It was all fun, though. Cruikshank in 1843 summed up what it meant to the man-in-the-street :

At the Surrey Menagerie everyone knows
(Because it's a place to which everyone goes)
There's a model of Rome : and as round it one struts
One sinks the remembrance of Newington Butts;
And having one's shilling laid down at the portal
One fancies oneself in the City Immortal!

A dinner at Soyer's Symposium at Gore House, Kensington in 1851. It was held for the Metropolitan Sanitary Association 'and the friends of Sanitary'. The paintings on the wall are by Madame Soyer. 'Chinese Lanterns, suspended from ceiling diffused a mellow and pleasant light over the brilliant pageant below and tables were decorated with a profusion of plate, rare exotics in vases and silvered mirror globes which multiplied and reflected the brilliant scene. A military band was in attendance, but concealed from view of the spectators and the gallery at the end of the hall was filled with ladies.'

The pleasure gardens were run on such an extravagant scale it was small wonder that they occasionally failed financially. The men who put up the money, hoping for a quick return, were sometimes disappointed, and the ownership of the pleasure gardens frequently changed. Some of the owners were not over scrupulous in their financial dealings and the land occupied by the gardens was becoming more and more valuable. The population was increasing, and towards the end of the century tall, stately houses were being erected on the sites. In place of the grass there were roads and pavements. Instead of the noise and crowds there was a well-bred peacefulness with only the occasional carriage, or the sound of a barrel organ in the distance to disturb it.

The New Towns

The sophistication and glamour of London was a magnet. There was so much to do, so much to see. The comparative dullness and solidity of the new towns in the provinces was in sharp contrast. People worked harder in the provinces—especially in the north—and the Saturday half-holiday was not general until the latter part of the century. A 10½-hour working day did not leave much time for entertainment, but what remained of the evenings could be enjoyed and there was, of course, Sunday.

The parks provided an opportunity for recreation where such games as ninepins, bowls and gymnastics could be enjoyed, and for the children there were roundabouts and swings. In the 1850s the free libraries were available—a refuge in the dark winter evenings from the discomforts of many a home and the weather outside. Most people were illiterate so the contents of the libraries appealed to a minority. Amongst the more popular books were *The Arabian Nights, Ivanhoe, Robinson Crusoe* and *Moll Flanders*, but even more in demand were histories about Napoleon and accounts of the lives of Wellington and Napoleon.

Before the free libraries there had been the Mechanics' Institute where, for 2 shillings a quarter, use could be made of the library and news-room. There were opportunities for sporting activities, too. 'Females' were admitted but hived off into different rooms where they could be taught the three 'Rs', sewing and knitting. Tea parties, concerts and soirées were also organised—sixpence being charged—and on occasions there were dances attended by as many as 700 people.

Many found entertainment in the pubs. The inhabitants reeled in and out of the public houses—there was one in Manchester for every eighty men and women of twenty years of age and older—and for those sober enough to enjoy it, there were music and sing-songs, acting, tumbling and dancing. Apples, oranges, ginger-beer, ale, porter and cigars—a 2d or 3d check at the entrance paid for all this and presumably more than one check could be bought. When the doors closed at night there were stalls in the street serving tripe and trotters liberally sprinkled with vinegar.

Sporting activities could hardly flourish in the over-crowded towns. Whippet-racing, pigeon-flying, prize-fighting took place in the mining villages and the open spaces where the rough Irishmen were building railways linking one industrial town with another.

The first Manchester Regatta was held in 1842, and there had been a cricket club at Bradford since 1836. By 1850 Birmingham boasted two cricket clubs and in about 1845 a suburban club—the Manchester Athenaeum—organised cricket, archery, quoits, fencing, boxing and single-stick. Most of these activities were confined to the 'middle classes', but a 'works' cricket team was not unknown. Those who preferred the more brutal sports had to go into the villages and surrounding country to find them.

Music—here again the middle-classes took the lead—became more popular. In Liverpool there were about a dozen halls in which concerts regularly took place. Soon after 1840 the Birmingham Musical Festival was launched and well-known artistes braved the journey from London to the industrial north to perform there. Hallé's orchestra in the Free Trade Hall during the 1850s was a feature of Manchester life attended by people who had travelled considerable distances in some discomfort and indifferent weather.

For the masses there was the brass band. Important contests between competing bands were held at the old Pomona Gardens near Manchester where the impressive amount of £50 was offered as a first prize. The annual band festival at Morpeth in Northumberland drew competitors from a wide area, and in Nelson, Lancashire, a band sponsored by a local cotton manufacturer secured prizes to the value of nearly £1,000 between 1870 and 1876.

In 1895 there were 222 brass band contests held in Great Britain, and so keen was the competition

Curling at the Ice Rink, Manchester, 1877

that some of the losers were not infused with the sporting spirit. On one occasion, it is recorded, the judge's comments were lost in a torrent of foul language coming from competing bandsmen and their friends who formed most of the audience, and an adjudicator was saved from serious assault at a railway station by the prompt intervention of the porters.

The theatre came a poor second. There was something basically wicked about even entering one and the theatres that existed were patronised by a middle-class public. Manchester possessed two theatres in 1860; the more sophisticated Liverpool had four. Seats could be bought for as little as 1 shilling for boxes, sixpence for the pit and threepence for the gallery, but at the Birmingham Royal when a well-known London company was performing the seat prices rocketed to 4 shillings for boxes, 3 shillings for upper boxes, pit 2 shillings and gallery 1 shilling—sums of money, it was pointed out, far out of reach of 'the sons of toil'. The 'sons of toil' preferred the public houses and the robustness of the music hall.

As in London, the 'palaces of variety' developed from humble origins. At first the entertainment took place in the tap rooms of public houses, and they were known as 'free-and-easies'. Another aspect was the Catch Club. Local men of wealth and influence would subscribe money each winter for hiring a hall and artistes for a series of concerts. The Dover Catch Club was one of the better known and some of the performers were 'big names' from London which added to the attraction. Generally though, the performers were well known and popular in the district, and it was from the Catch Club that the smoking concert developed.

1850

Life in the new provincial towns was mostly work with little time for play. Sunday—the only full day of rest—was to be taken seriously. Rest was essential. It had been a hard week. The mill hands toiled long hours and so did the office boys; there was little to choose between the conditions under which they worked. Factories and offices—both could be insanitary and derelict, and often were.

On Sunday the families made their way to church. The less religious spent the day drinking and sleeping off the effects. It was only on Sundays, when the factory furnaces were stilled, that the sun, penetrating the smoke-laden gloom, shone weakly on the people of the new towns and cities.

In the villages the winters must have seemed long and cold. Distance prevented people from visiting each other, but when there was a party at one of the houses it became an 'occasion'. The girls wore white frocks with blue sashes. Hair was brushed, faces scrubbed no matter what objections were made at the time. When ready, all assembled in the hall shivering with cold and excitement. The governess in charge would open the front door and peer outside. When the carriage was at the door everyone crowded in and the slow ride to the house where the party was being held began. On arrival it must have taken some time to thaw out, and when it was time to return home again it might well be foggy. Then a footman, with a lantern held high above his head, his coat buttoned up to his nose, would lead the way by walking in front of the carriage.

Except at Christmas, parties were few and far between. Christmas was the longed-for occasion, the highlight of activity and excitement. An entire family might take over the village hall, and from the stage came a wide variety of entertainment. The boys recited 'John Peel' or 'Hearts of Oak' followed by the piping voices of the girls rendering 'Casabianca' and 'The Village Blacksmith'. The youngest members of the family—wrapped warmly in Shetland shawls but shivering from nerves—would wait for their cue. Then, with varying degrees of confidence familiar nursery rhymes would be enacted. After the applause and inevitable encore, the governess might take her place at the piano; at her side a young girl with a violin. A smile of reassurance from the governess, an 'I'm-ready-to-start' nod and a duet would begin uncertainly, either gaining in competence as it progressed, or racking the nerves of the well-intentioned audience.

Christmas over, life resumed its settled ways with lessons for the children; but there was much of the day to be filled in. The pets had to be looked after—rabbits, tortoises, a pony—and in the dark evenings there were books to read or stories to be told. A gentle game, perhaps, a collection of shells to be arranged, or flowers to be pressed, but before it was dark there was always the organised afternoon walk to be completed. Daily at luncheon a basket would be filled by the lady of the house with what was left over from the table. This was taken to the poor and provided and excellent excuse for a walk as it was possible to glow inwardly with goodness and outwardly with exercise. The poor were always there; so were the sick, the lame and the blind. All needed visiting at least once a week. Mothers with new-born children were supplied with gruel and the loan of a 'bag' from which they might select any clothing they needed.

In the main, entertainment was within the community. Miss Mitford, writing of village life in early Victorian days, had these observations to make:

> Of all situations for a constant residence that which appears to me most delightful is a little village far in the country; a small neighbourhood, not of fine mansions finely peopled, but of cottages and cottage-like houses . . . with inhabitants whose faces are familiar to us as the flowers in our gardens; a little world of our own, close-packed and insulated like ants in an ant-hill, or bees in a hive . . . where we know every one, are known to every one, interested in every one, and authorised to hope that every one feels an interest in us.

Improved communications broke up this idyllic picture of village life, and ever since—despite all the 'entertainment' as we know it today—people have been striving unsuccessfully to return to the peace and simplicity of the Victorian village which Miss Mitford found so enchanting.

Village life : entertaining the poor

Songs and Supper—
the Music Hall Years

The Song and Supper Rooms were much frequented in the early part of the Queen's reign. There, well served, hot suppers could be obtained up to the early hours of the morning. Stout and hot grog were poured down many throats, and smoke from cigars hung heavily over the proceedings which consisted of vocalists—sentimental and comic—employed by the management. Talented customers, suitably primed with drinks, dared to venture on to the platform to sing a song or give a recitation.

The best known Song and Supper Rooms were the Cyder Cellars in Maiden Lane, the Coal Hole in the Strand, Offley's in Henrietta Street, the Dr Johnson in Bolt Court off Fleet Street, and Evans's (later to become Paddy Green's) in Covent Garden (number 43 King Street).

Mr John Greenmore (known as Paddy Green) took over Evans's in 1844 and spent about £5,000 in decoration and reconstruction. The walls were lined with pictures of celebrated theatrical personalities and there was a screened gallery extending along two sides and one end of the hall. Ladies were admitted on conditions. One was that they had to give their name and address; the other was that when they were admitted they could sit only in the screened gallery.

On the stage an all-male cast appeared. A choir of men and boys sang ballads, glees and madrigals with popular selections from operas, all to the accompaniment of a piano and a harmonium.

The show began at 8 o'clock in the evening but the place did not fill up until later. By midnight it was difficult to find a table. Famous figures in the world of art, literature (it was a short walk from the Garrick Club for Thackeray) and the professions could be seen talking splendidly and consuming chops washed down with strong stout.

Presiding over the proceedings was Paddy Green himself, red-faced, benevolent, chatting to his distinguished guests and taking copious pinches of snuff.

J. W. Sharp the comedian, known as Jack Sharp, sang his songs, 'The Cockney Tourist or Where Shall We Go To?' and 'Cab! Cab! Cabby!'

> I'm what they calls a 'Cabby',
> And once I got took in
> By a gent so precious shabby,
> What hadn't got no tin.
> Round Evans I plied,
> When a tipsy gent I spied.
> 'Cab, Cab,' says he,
> 'Drive like a brick
> To Highgate, t'other side.'

The song continues for numerous verses during which the tipsy gent orders the cabby to take him to Camberwell, Regent's Park and elsewhere. When the gent eventually gets out he says he's dropped a sovereign in the cab, but the poor cabby never finds it. Sam Cowell was another star at Evans's. His famous songs included 'Black Your Boots' and 'The Rat-catcher's Daughter'. Harry Sydney was popular with his 'I'm a Young Man from the Country but you Don't Get Over Me'.

The audience was requested—or rather 'respectfully' requested—'to encourage the vocalists by attention, the Cafe part of the rooms being intended for Conversational Parties'.

The Variety Saloon differed from the Song and Supper Room. It was licensed by the magistrates and in the premises it was permitted to stage any kind of entertainment, except Shakespearean drama. There would be a mixture of opera, drama and farce with music and dancing to finish the evening off. The Eagle in the City Road was a Variety Saloon.

> Up and down the City Road,
> In and out the Eagle,
> That's the way the money goes—
> Pop goes the weasel.

The Eagle, or the Grecian Saloon as it was sometimes called, had all the appearances of a theatre—stage, tiers of boxes, an organ back stage which was hidden by a cloth when drama was performed. When ballet became popular the organ was taken away and an orchestra substituted.

Other Variety Saloons were the Union, Shoreditch; the Apollo, Marylebone; the Bower in Stangate Street, Lower Marsh; the Albert in Shepherdess Walk, and the Effingham in the Whitechapel Road.

What terminated the Variety Saloons was the passing of the Theatres Registry Act in 1843 which confronted the proprietors under licence with a difficult choice. Either they could run a legitimate theatre without refreshments in the auditorium, or they could become music halls where drinks could be served, but stage plays could not be put on. Some of the saloons became variety theatres and others staged plays.

From the Variety Saloons followed the Tavern Concert Rooms which were the forerunners of the music hall. The Grapes in Southwark; the Mogul in Drury Lane; the King's Head, Knightsbridge were a few of the countless Concert Rooms which existed in all parts of London. At them appeared the rank and file of the variety profession whose names were to shine in lights in later years. The sentimental vocalist, the male impersonator, the comic singer, the Ethiopian minstrel, the ventriloquist, the tap-dancer—all served their apprenticeship at the Concert Rooms.

It was from these beginnings that the music hall developed. At the music hall the working classes found a refuge from the reality of their drab lives. It was an improvement on the eighteenth-century tavern. When the Canterbury Hall was opened by the enterprising Charles Morton in 1852, the ladies were admitted every evening instead of on specific 'ladies' nights' as in the past.

On payment of 6d the visitor was given a refreshment ticket with which he purchased food although at a later date an additional 3d was charged.

Inside the Canterbury the balcony extended round the room in the shape of a horseshoe. On the platform was a piano and a harmonium played between the acts). Below the stage sat the chairman who announced the turns and generally compèred the show. It was his duty to keep order which was not always easy with a 'tough' audience. The audience—in the main—consisted of hard-working people: tradesmen, warehousemen, clerks and their womenfolk. The hall was heavy with smoke and the thick smell of beer.

The more sleazy music halls were drab. The entrance might be through a shop, the admission a penny which was exchanged for a metal check. Visitors passed through the hall, the walls crumbling, ill-lit by gas. At the counter were non-intoxicating drinks and the opportunity for a mild flutter at a gaming-table.

Once in the hall—which might hold a thousand—the sexes were separated. In front of the stage sat a fiddler and a harpist. When they and the artistes were ready, a man illuminated the footlights consisting of several gas jets coming from a rusty pipe running the length of the stage.

By then the audience showed impatience. The stamping of feet and clapping of hands made it essential that the curtain should rise—which it did in a series of convulsive jerks.

The first turn might be grand opera—burlesqued and entirely vocal. First to appear on the stage is the Deserted Wife who, in a sad little tune, bewails her plight. Enter the Husband who cheerfully acknowledges he has enjoyed the gay life. His Deserted Wife tells him where to get off, and she is

49

'If you travel the Continent over,
The Rhine, Sir, above and below,
You'll find it not safe for the present
The Tour of all Europe to go. . . .
Oh, where shall a traveller go,
Oh, where can a tourist now go? . . .
From Constantinople to Dover
There's nowhere a tourist can go.'

A tavern music hall, 1856. The Lord Nelson in Whitechapel

accused by him of jealousy. Nothing *he* can do, she says, could make *her* jealous. The Husband puts her to the test by singing the praises of the Other Woman. The Deserted Wife, in a frenzy of operatic hysteria, bewails her circumstances. Suddenly the Husband sees the evil of his ways and announces that the Other Woman never existed, and anyhow he won't see her again. The Wife, no longer Deserted, is re-united with her Husband and a happy-ever-after duet rings down—in jerks—the curtain.

Backstage the scene is being changed and in the process the audience can hear the noise that this entails. When the curtain jerks up again an athletic-looking man is on the stage. He has as props a bowl, decanters half-filled with wine, and some chairs. The finale is when he places each leg of a chair on a decanter. On this chair he places another, upside down. He then leaps to the top of the upside-down chair and stands on his head. It would be a blasé audience that failed to respond to such an act as this, and the applause rings out.

The next act is something of a star turn. A singer, well dressed and with a commanding presence that enables him to order the orchestra (of two) to strike up the opening bars of a comic song. Once launched the singer explains he is a thief—but not of the petty variety. On the contrary (he sings), he dines with a lord and sups with the lord's servant, and he robs both. This is very well received.

Lastly there is a ballet, the main characters—in the pantomime tradition—are Columbine and Pantaloon, the comic Spooney and the hated Rival.

The songs of the music halls reflected the attitudes of the audience who were often burdened with debts and living in the poorest circumstances. A song, sung to the tune of 'Green Grows the Rushes'

The 'Oxford', 1861

and entitled 'The Daily News', expressed the thoughts of many members of the audience in a cynical way. The chorus is quoted here:

> The newspapers are all my eye,
> So don't the *Times* or *Sun* peruse;
> Just listen to me, and I'll try
> To tell you what's the daily news.
> The daily news is this, my boys—
> The rich get richer every day,
> Monopolising all life's joys,
> While the poor the piper have to pay.
> French cooks and tailors for the great,
> For the small hard fare and oft no shoes;
> And hundreds forced to emigrate—
> That's *bona-fide* daily news.

By 1868 there were 28 music halls in London and 300 in the rest of the country. In Sheffield there were 10, Birmingham had 9, Manchester and Leeds 8 each. They varied in comfort and decor, but to eat, drink and be merry in a friendly atmosphere fulfilled a need. Favourite dishes were pease pudding and trotters, a dozen oysters with bread and butter (for 1 shilling), or a good, solid portion of steak and kidney with potatoes in their jackets. A five-course meal at the Oxford Music Hall at the corner of Tottenham Court Road (including the entertainment that went with it) cost half-a-crown.

By 1870 famous theatres such as the London Pavilion, Sam Collins' Music Hall, The Holborn, Alhambra, Metropolitan, Middlesex, Gatti's Hall of Varieties, were all doing good business, and in the eighties came the New Tivoli, the Empire and others.

The demand for artistes increased and the ladies came into their own: Annie Adams singing 'Are you Gazing on this little Beauty' and Kate Harley—one of the first to appear in male attire—with 'Away down Holborn Hill'.

It is the old-timers that people remember: Dan Leno, Tom Costello, Harry Randall, Charles Coburn, Little Tich. Their patter, their songs and their professionalism delighted audiences who came to see them time and time again. The juggler, the conjuror, dancers, acrobats—all were needed to make up the programme.

It was obvious, though, that standards of safety and cleanliness hardly existed. Many too many people were crowded into unsuitable buildings. In 1878 the authorities in London were required to issue a 'Certificate of Suitability' before a licence could be given or renewed. Surveys of existing music hall buildings revealed serious structural defects which proprietors could not afford to put right. Under certain circumstances a safety curtain was insisted upon, but it was more than the proprietor could afford, and the weight was more than many structures could stand.

The authorities held the view that liquor was better outside the auditorium than inside. Consequently bars open to the auditorium with a 'promenade' between were permitted, but later the sale of liquor was separated entirely from the auditorium. The tables and chairs in the auditorium were removed altogether and seats substituted. The audience sat in the auditorium to see the show; for refreshment they had to go elsewhere in the building.

Many of the music halls had to close and the new regulations inaugurated a fresh era. The taverns and the saloons were on the way out. In their place was built the lavish variety theatre, solid in marble, softly carpeted, dazzlingly lit by electricity. No longer was such entertainment confined to the poor and the needy. The elegance of the new variety theatres attracted wealth and fashion. The music hall 'chairman' disappeared. The hard chairs were replaced by luxurious tip-up seats.

Performances were once nightly with a matinée on Saturday afternoon. Belmont's Music Hall in Hackney Road was the first to institute twice-nightly shows in 1885, but it was not until the next

Evans's in Covent Garden. A brilliant scene in 1856 when it was reconstructed in part. The lighting was gas.

The Canterbury in Lambeth, 1856. The hall could hold 1,000 people an evening.

century that this became normal practice.

In the 1880s there were fashionable, lavish variety theatres in London's West End; the smaller, less lavish music halls were away from Piccadilly Circus but still in the West End; large music halls were established in the suburbs, and finally dingy music halls were to be found in the poor districts.

The hey-day of the variety theatre was during the reign of Edward VII. In the last years of the nineteenth century the stage was set for a more sophisticated and less rumbustious entertainment favoured by Oswald Stoll who acquired a number of halls, joined forces with Edward Moss and Richard Thornton to form the Moss Empire of variety theatres which was to influence entertainment up to World War I.

In 1896 the first cinematograph was shown at the Empire, Leicester Square. The 'bioscope' of news and events became part of a variety programme. This, more than anything else, was to signal the decline of flesh-and-blood entertainment as the Victorians knew it.

Playing the Game

Epsom Races—the Return from the Derby, 1843,
—those who made it, those who enjoyed

portrays a panorama of Victorian entertainment
who had had a bad day and were not amused.

Until the latter part of the nineteenth century, sport was disorganised. Depending on the social standing of the participant, money and time spent on sport varied enormously. At the one end there was the country house, a setting for splendour and gracious living where life revolved round the pack of hounds and the hunters in the stables. The duke or the squire had his own pack and it was expected that visitors to the estate should want to hunt too. The etiquette of the hunting field had to be acquired at an early age and the Master's children, it was pointed out in one instance, never hunted more than three times a week until they were five years old.

There was no area of land over which it was forbidden to hunt—after all the Master owned the land —and the tenants and farm-workers (in the Master's employ) showed a healthy respect when hounds, horses and riders thundered past. The hunting field was the Master's domain. The financial upkeep of the hunt was often his personal responsibility. It was the occasion of meeting and greeting one's friends and entertaining them on a grand scale which was all the more deserved after the exhilarating exercise of a hard day's hunting.

Friends were tested in the hunting field. Their behaviour in hunting pink coloured their characters and stamina. The hunt was open to all, provided, of course, they knew the rules and were socially

The Squire

58

Cat among the 'pigeons'. The shoot.

acceptable, which included the sporting parson and perhaps the doctor, but excluded the local tradesmen.

A topic of conversation was the colourful exploits of famous huntsmen and steeplechasers such as George Osbaldeston and Jack Mytton. The wagers, the challenges, their eating and drinking capacities —all this was mulled over in the taverns and hilariously discussed round the well-appointed tables of country gentlemen. The older these almost legendary figures became, the less inclined they were to 'let up'. Red of face and short of breath they might be, but it was important that their image of eternal youth should not fade. It might be preferable to die suddenly endeavouring to repeat an exploit of one's youth, than to linger into old age with only memories of past achievements.

The hunting, shooting, fishing of the country gentleman was pursued undisturbed in peaceful, luxurious surroundings. There is an impression of continuous coming and going of royalty and friends, a perpetual weekend of sunshine, talk and good food and splendid drinking. There appeared to be no organised entertainment; it was a way of life. Surely it must continue for ever?

The growth of cricket, soccer and Rugby football, rowing and athletics was fostered to some extent by the public schools which were increasing in number during the 1840s and 1850s. It was the schools and universities which decreed what games were to be played and, more important, how they were to be played. The games 'cult' flourished, and in such an atmosphere proficiency at sport was to be preferred to the 'swot' who failed to shine at it. The old public schoolboy and the young man down from university often took an active part in bringing some sort of order into a sport lacking the most elementary rules. The formation, for example, of the Football Association in 1863 was largely due to such efforts.

Officers of the 93rd Highlanders and their game trophies. c 1864

Football satisfied the aggressive instincts of the young mill workers and coal miners cooped up in confined spaces for most of their lives. All that was needed was a plot of ground, a street even. A ball thrown in the air was caught or kicked and a wild rush ensued to get possession of it. As late as 1880 —on Shrove Tuesday—the streets of Dorking in Surrey were the scene of a match between the towns-folk. For obstructing the highway and endangering life, some fifty participants were fined a shilling plus costs by the magistrates. Excursion trains steamed into Workington disgorging thousands of passengers who had come to see four or five hundred men, stripped to the waist, floundering in slime. Occasionally the ball was sighted and a concerted attempt was made to grab it. If—as it might—the ball landed in the street a roar went up and the 'game' was continued in the centre of the town if needs be. No holds were barred, few fences were left intact, walls were climbered over and battles were fought in the back yards of peaceful citizens.

Cricket flourished on the village green and there were keen matches between parishes. It was the day of the amateur who, because he had private means, could afford to spend all the summer playing. County cricket was strong in the southern counties but was accepted in the north less readily. In 1870 regular county fixtures numbered twenty-two; eight years later there were as many as 188. In the north, piece-workers on the looms who were the most enthusiastic cricketers could take time off during the day to give themselves a game and recoup the wages lost by working on a Sunday.

Conditions at the grounds were not too comfortable. The pitches at the Oval, Canterbury, Brighton and Fenner's were good, but at Lord's it was stated that the only parts of a billiard table the pitch resembled were the pockets. On many grounds there were no facilities for the players to have lunch. They joined in the struggle with the spectators for beer and sandwiches.

It was the period of great cricketers. The halcyon years for the amateur were between 1860 and 1880 when the great figures, a little larger than life, dominated the scene.

The immense sums of money wagered on the race course encouraged the most appalling frauds in which the aristocracy were deeply involved. Sophisticated doping of horses was unknown, but cruder methods such as poisoning the drinking water, were effective. Owners and jockeys with large sums of money at stake conspired to hold back mounts or substitute them; age limits were faked, races started unpunctually, and weighing-in and weighing-out were carelessly attended to. Lord George Bentinck and Admiral J. H. Rous took active steps to reform the sport which had become disreputable. The Jockey Club's influence had, since 1750, been confined to Newmarket. Now it was to become the supreme authority for all racing throughout Great Britain.

Through the eighteenth and most of the nineteenth centuries cock-fighting was a sport indulged in by kings and princes as well as by the rough inhabitants of the rural districts. It was brutal, and an Act of 1849 suppressed it. A year later there was the 'greatest meeting ever held in England' between Norfolk and Suffolk. An Easter meeting at the Gallowgate Pit, Newcastle in the same year attracted 300 entries.

In 1875 at Brawnton there was a match between Paignton and Alnwick with every precaution taken against interference from the law. At a Preston meeting the mayor was one of the spectators. The sudden arrival of the police placed him in a predicament, so to escape he hid in a chimney. His girth

Yorkshire v Lancashire, 1890

Sayers v Heenan near Farnborough, 1860. In order to avoid the unwelcome attention
of the police, the ring was concealed in a dip.

prevented him concealing himself entirely but the police, recognising the dignitary's nether regions,
left him where he was.

The popularity of professional pugilism was at its height in the classic match between Sayers and
Heenan in 1860. So as to avoid the unwelcome attention of the police, tickets were available at £5
bearing the cryptic words 'There and Back'. The place where the fight was to take place was known
only to prominent members of the 'fancy'. Under a cloak of secrecy whispered instructions were
given. On arrival at a 'certain' station a train was boarded which travelled a roundabout route until it
reached Farnborough. There the passengers left the train and scampered over fields, fences and walls
to reach the ring which was suitably situated for concealment and viewing. The contest lasted two
hours and the result was 'no decision' due to the arrival of the police. There then followed a scene
of such confusion in the ring that prize fighting was degraded to an extent that the Sayers and Heenan fight became the last classic battle. The brutality and dishonesty that attended such contests could
no longer be tolerated by men of honour. It was no longer a 'sport'. It attracted the worst elements.
Even after prize fighting became illegal it continued. The selected place needed to be secluded and it
was equally important that the spot fixed upon was on the borders of two counties. When the police
of one county appeared the spectators and contestants moved over the border and resumed the contest out of harm's way.

Sir Robert Peel's newly formed police force was confronted with problems which its lack of co-
ordination did nothing to solve. The favoured place for a prize fight was near Birmingham where the
three counties of Warwickshire, Staffordshire and Worcester were adjacent. If the police were not
mobile the spectators certainly were, and at the first sign of trouble the ropes and stakes were

gathered up and an impromptu ring erected in one of the counties where the police were unaware of what was going on.

Although women enjoyed taking part in sport they received little encouragement from the men. When women invaded the sacred realm of golf, their club house was tucked away in a quiet corner so that the men had no need to be contaminated. Women were physically unsuited for sport, thought men, and their dress hampered such activities. Archery was a woman's sport and they were patronisingly accepted as tennis players. A game of croquet was to be encouraged—the setting of the game fitted the vision of a gentle Victorian lady although the game itself, properly played, dispelled such an image. On the whole, though, the important business of Playing the Game must be left to the men for which, of course, they were admirably equipped.

There was a rumour that in 1878 a lady cyclist had actually accompanied her husband on a tour of the countryside. For some years only a tricycle was considered suitable for a lady to ride, although the introduction of the tandem 'where a lady was induced to take the front seat under masculine convoy and protection' was acceptable.

Even in the eighties a woman on a bicycle was considered a curious and unedifying spectacle. One of the difficulties was to find somewhere sufficiently secluded away from prying eyes where ladies could learn to ride. Those fortunate enough to have a large secluded garden could practise there, but for some only the open road was available very early in the morning before people were out and about.

When the Boat Race really meant something. Hammersmith Bridge, c 1872

At Croquet, Croquet, a proper game to play,
At Croquet, Croquet, I could play all day,
There's nothing can surpass, the sport upon the grass
In that Awfully Jolly game call'd Croquet.

A HUNT BREAKFAST AT HOLLYBUSH (Meet of the 'Flintstone Foxhounds')

Rather a penance for Mr Hockington, 'the master', who is not a 'society' man, and hates this sort of thing. He tilts a chair up and down on its hind legs, and listens as patiently as he can to Sir Robert Reynardson's account of a famous run with the Flintstone, when *he* was master, twenty years ago.

Sir Hector is welcoming Mrs Doggins of Draggerham, who has just arrived with her well 'got-up', but rather stupid-looking husband. (Mrs D is the great lady-rider of the Flintstone, hunting five days a week, to the discomfort of her household, and, one would fancy, utter neglect of her family.)

Lady Mopus is doing the honours among the other lady visitors.

Mr Weather and the guests stopping in the house, have all breakfasted early and are gossiping with the fresh arrivals, while the Rev. Horace Hoodwink does ample justice to the cutlets at the corner-table, his appetite, no doubt, sharpened by the canter from Cassock Bridge, nine miles off, on his clever cob.

— from *Holly Bush Hall* by Georgina Bowers, 1871

E

1878—Ashington in Sussex: a country cricket match. (Painting by J. R. Reid—1851-1926.)

66

A Decent 'Drop'

A macabre entertainment was the public hanging. Outside the prison gates up to 1868 it was usual for a large crowd to assemble in order to see a decent 'drop'. Women with children were in evidence and refreshments were served by street traders.

When Rush was executed for the Stanfield Hall murder in 1849 a special train arrived at Norwich disgorging a crowd of sightseers from London. At Stafford jail in 1839 James Owen and George Thomas, convicted of the wilful murder of Christine Collins, drew an almost unprecedented audience —nearly ten thousand. Every spot, remote and near, from which a view of the 'drop' could be obtained, was occupied. Walls, trees, the roofs of houses were popular vantage points and the three roads approaching the jail were filled with people as far as the eye could see. It was recorded that 'no peculiar feeling was displayed when the men made their appearance on the drop; though when it fell the females, who were very numerous, gave partial vent to their emotions'.

In rural Bodmin in 1840 James and William Lightfoot were convicted of the murder of a Mr Norway, a timber merchant living at Wadebridge. About ten thousand people saw the men, pale but collected, walk with a firm step and ascend the ladder unassisted. Before being placed on the 'drop' they shook hands with those in attendance and thanked the clergyman. When the 'drop' fell there was little emotion exhibited and the inhabitants of Cornwall were doubtless content that they had collected nearly £3,500 for the impoverished widow and family of the murdered man.

It was James Payn who pointed out that it was not the hanging of the criminals that was the worst part of an execution, but the behaviour of the mob. Having paid 20 guineas for a room overlooking the scene at Newgate, he took his place there at 3 o'clock one winter's morning. First the scaffold arrived painted black, and drawn by three cart-horses. Furious knocking and hammering followed and the gallows were erected, by which time the snow began to fall. At dawn the crowds extended as far as the eye could see. Hats were not permitted because they obscured the view. Improvised headgear, colourful and weird, was worn instead. The white caps of the bakers, the blue caps of the soldiers and the black caps of the chimney sweeps were to be seen. By way of a diversion the sweeps were encouraged to slap one another so that the soot flew freely over those standing close to them. It was not unusual for men to leap upon the shoulders of those near to them and make their way on all fours along the top of the crowd in order to be closer to the scene.

Women were present—mostly young girls—and Payn observed 'no touch of pity, or even of awe, could be read in any countenance'. When a black cloth, about two feet high was placed round the edge of the scaffold there were cries of fury from the crowd as the sight of the bodies being lowered into the coffins would be obscured.

Shortly before 8 o'clock the arrival of the hangman provoked some cheers. Carefully he examined the equipment. Then the bell of St Sepulchre's boomed and there were cries of 'Hats off' so that everyone should see. At the prison door stood a posse of officials. An instant later five men emerged and began their walk to the scaffold. Payn writes that the crowd of 40,000 emitted 'a certain purring satisfaction, like that of a cat over its prey'. Then a sharp hiss was heard and a shout of 'Cur' because one of the victims had fainted and needed to sit down. There were cheers for those who walked to their doom 'with as jaunty an air as his pinioned arms will permit'.

The priest spoke; the victims, through the hoods over their heads, kissed the crucifix. Throughout it all the crowd babbled on. 'Only after a certain dreadful grinding noise,' writes Payn, 'which is the fall of the drop—a flood of uproar suddenly bursts forth, which must have been pent up before.' He adds, 'Singularly enough, the crowd increased after the execution, persons of delicate temperament joining it, I suppose, who had not nerve enough for a hanging, but who knew how to appreciate a cutting down'.

The Victorian's interest in crime continued long after public executions were abolished in 1868. The era had its fair share of notorious criminals and sensational trials. The words 'notorious' and 'sensational' have now been debased, but at a time when news was confined to the press the words really meant what they said. Even more delectable were the court scenes involving high society such as the Tranby Croft slander case in which the Prince of Wales was called as witness; the Oscar Wilde trial; and also the long drawn-out Tichborne trial which occupied the courts for almost three years, cost the State the best part of £100,000, and drew the comment from *Punch*:

> Unto boredom's highest niche borne,
> There enshrine the name of Tichborne.

Outside Newgate, 1848

Warder showing visitors plaster casts of the heads of criminals hanged at Newgate, 1873.

The Social Round

The fashionable, wealthy young woman hunted, rode and skated. Not even the London season, when she danced the hours away from dusk to dawn, could prevent her indulging in a favourite sport. At the end of the season a visit to a fashionable resort enabled her to swim and play tennis for four or five hours a day although the constant change from running about in the sun and cooling off in the shade was to the 'imminent risk of her health and the ruin of her complexion'.

Then to Scotland, striding over moors with the grouse-shooters or sitting 'beside her friends partridge driving, occasionally trying her hand at a shot'. Came the winter when, weather permitting, meals out of doors and 'a long drag through the coverts or over turnips and perhaps a dance to finish up the evening'. No wonder living at such a pace some girls broke down after a couple of seasons.

At the country clubs at Ranelagh and Hurlingham the men played polo or competed in pony races. For the women, watching it could be deadly dull although the alternative—sitting at home waiting for

Ascot, 1844

A LAMENT.

Dowager. "It's been the worst Season I can remember, Sir-James! All the Men seem to have got Married, and none of the Girls!"

1884

visitors—was to be avoided at all costs. Thoughts were occupied with what to wear on the numerous different occasions. The fashionable race meetings—Newmarket, Ascot, Epsom, Goodwood—required a very comprehensive wardrobe and a decision could be based on the advice given by a writer of the period as to the fashion ratio: 'Newmarket, great; Goodwood, greater; Ascot, greatest'.

After Goodwood, Cowes and the regatta week, with dances, sailing, small impromptu dinners and an opportunity for 'ravishing dresses, sailor hats, coquettish yachting headgear, and a general air of freshness and workmanlike appearance which is peculiarly appropriate to English girls'.

Impressive functions were held at Almack's in King Street, St James's. Almack's—which opened in the eighteenth century and flourished until the 1860s—consisted of rooms let to the elite for a variety of social functions. Each Wednesday night, throughout the London season, Almack's was the scene of an Assembly Ball organised by titled ladies. It was difficult to obtain admission. It was not enough to have the mere 7s 6d for a ticket. Those who had failed to get born with a canteen of silver spoons in the mouth, or had acquired wealth through 'trade', were not considered suitable. Social standing and impeccable behaviour were of paramount importance and nobody could be sure they would be admitted however socially 'acceptable' they might be in other quarters. The titled ladies, who dispensed the admittance tickets, were aware of many well-bred skeletons in the cupboards of some of the applicants.

Application had to be made in writing and a messenger had to be sent for the reply. Those favoured with tickets had to pay particular attention to their dress. Any diversion from what was considered fashionable and correct could result in the guests being turned away. Once admitted, the great staircase had to be successfully negotiated. Critical eyes watched every step. The ballroom, with its gilt

71

Eton v Harrow at Lord's, 1878

columns, medallions and mirrors was dazzlingly lit by gas. In such a setting the cream of Victorian society danced the waltz, the quadrille, Caledonians, mazurka or the daring polka, to the music of Weippert's famous band.

Somehow the excess of food and drink had to be worked off. Hyde Park's Rotten Row where one could ride in the company of a beautiful woman (or good-looking man) was a very pleasant way of exercising. The riders were elegantly attired. A canter enabled one to see and to be seen; a gallop might be conspicous and it attracted too much attention to the horse. There was always the possibility of disaster, such as falling off.

To see and be seen was also the object of the afternoon drive in Hyde Park. It mattered with whom one shared the carriage. It was, naturally, of the utmost importance what one was wearing. Tongues wagged and conclusions—often the wrong ones were drawn. Gossip flourished under such conditions. All this could be enjoyed by the lowly without any of the social responsibilities. To those not in the social swim it was entertaining to watch the carriages go by with the elegant passengers inside. With good fortune it might be possible to obtain a glimpse of Queen Victoria and Prince Albert. The sidewalks were frequented by nurses with their charges, and small boys cleverly manipulating hoops so that collisions with pedestrians were just avoided. Dandies, dressed in the fashion of the day with incredible waistcoats and colourful ties, focussed field glasses on the personalities as they went by.

It was the English Sunday that could be the dullest, heaviest day. In the country it was fairly easily disposed of. Church in the morning—that was inevitable—and after church a chair in the garden in

AMENITIES OF THE TENNIS-LAWN.

She. "YOURS OR MINE, SIR CHARLES?"   *He.* "YOURS—AW'FLY YOURS!"

CES AUTRES "

(HEARD AT CHURCH-PARADE.)

Captain Bergamot. "ARE ANY OF YOUR BROTHERS IN THE SERVICE, MISS DE BULLION?"
Miss de Bullion. "YES; ONE IN THE GUARDS, AND—A—" (*with disgust*)—"THE REST IN THE COMMON ARMY, YOU KNOW."

The Royal Academy, c 1870

which one could recline well propped up with cushions, hat tilted over the eyes for protection from the sun which always seemed to be shining. If female, one squinted (attractively) at the handsome young men of the party as they entered the garden, and made one's tactical dispositions accordingly. If successful the one of your choice might sit on the grass at your feet. All he needed was an occasional brandy-and-soda or lemon squash and on that relationship it is recorded 'the fair sex invaded the regimental drags, the paddocks and saddling enclosures, the once sacred precincts of Tattersall, and even the smoking-rooms of country houses'.

After lunch a stroll round the stables to admire your host's horses. With good fortune the young man of the morning might accompany you, and when the equestrian small talk was over there was a good chance he would ask you to play tennis with him, or pick strawberries or gooseberries in the garden.

Sunday in London lacked such pleasures. After church, Church Parade in Hyde Park where the newest dresses, the most daring hats were shown to best advantage. Sunday lunch—so tedious because it rarely finished before four o'clock in the afternoon—hardly enabled one to do justice to the dinner that followed in the evening.

When the air became oppressive and it was no longer possible to stand another whole Sunday in London, those in the know took the 10.30 train from Paddington in the morning and later, on reaching Maidenhead, languished by the river. White flannels and punts, snatches of conversation coming to you across the water, and delightful hours spent in the shade of the drooping willow trees made a tedious Sunday into a day that was not only bearable but actually pleasant.

On the way to Henley, c 1887

MID-WINTER

A large party come to Hollybush, for skating on the river.

Maude detests the ice, but is persuaded by Major Myrtle to try one turn in his wife's skates.

Charlie Cleve and Kate Reynardson, cut all sorts of figures hand-in-hand, and Nevill Hawke comes down from town, for the day, in a frightfully unbecoming seal-skin cap.

Mrs Dogins of Draggerham drives her ponies over in a sleigh, and sits for an age listening, patiently, to dear old Sir Hector's prosing, rather than interfere with what she fancies a promising flirtation between her sister and Lord Curragh, who stands behind her carriage.

—from *Holly Bush Hall* by Georgina Bowers, 1871

The Quest for the Moving Picture

The magic lantern—invented in the seventeenth century—became an important entertainment in public and private. A wide variety of slides on all manner of subjects was available and there were devices enabling an animated image to be shown on the screen. The slides were hand-drawn or painted up to 1880, after which engravings and drawings were transferred to slides by photographic methods and then coloured. Consequently the quality of the picture projected deteriorated.

As an alternative to flesh and blood, the magic lantern enabled people to see the world. Foreign countries became more real, scientific subjects could be demonstrated, the wonders of the world could be shown in all their colourful glory. At parties in the home the magic lantern was used to while away some of the time, and a programme such as the following was offered:

A COUNTRY COTTAGE BY DAY—Evening (moonlight night)—Winter comes with falling snow. (The various changes are made imperceptibly giving a most natural effect.)

MYSTIFY & CO (An original fairy tale, illustrated by beautiful hand-painted pictures with rapid changes and illusions.)

THE HOUSES OF PARLIAMENT (with moon appearing and ripples on the water).

THE HOTEL DE VILLE, PARIS (with charming effect by lighting up each window).

'THE PIED PIPER OF HAMLIN'. (This well-known poem has been shortened and illustrated by a very clever artist.)

Then followed Flower Studies demonstrating the new process of 'Photography in Colours', and Animal Studies at the Zoo. Afterwards a recitation ('illustrated most humorously') entitled 'How Bill Adams won the Battle of Waterloo', a reading from Tennyson, and Stories for Children with 'various comic and amusing pictures all free from any objectionable feature'. The final item was 'Portraits of the Royal Family and Eminent Persons'. The National Anthem concluded the proceedings.

The Panorama—attributed to Robert Barker in the late eighteenth century—was a picture affixed to a large canvas attached to the inside of a rotunda which revolved slowly round the spectators seated in the centre. There were rotundas in London in the early part of the Queen's reign, but a more sophisticated variation was the Diorama devised by Jacques Daguerre (of daguerreotype fame). This was a three-dimensional contrivance and Daguerre's London Diorama was opened in Park Square East, Regent's Park in 1823. Two panoramas were produced—for the first time—from photographs of battles taken during the Crimean War. In the 1890s a programme depicting a journey from Niagara to London was seen by over a million people in a year. The performance was at 10-22 York Street, Westminster and the additional attractions were electric light, the 'building properly warmed', music and 'Colossal Panorama of the Great Falls'. Admission was a shilling and for no extra charge one could remain to see a 'Panoramic View of Southern cotton fields in full work'.

Elsewhere a 'veteran and only known rank-and-file survivor of the great battle' (of Waterloo) was an added attraction of a panorama of the event.

The first motion picture performance in England was given at the Regent Street Polytechnic in 1896 and in the same year the Empire music hall included a programme to an astonished audience in the smoking-lounge. It was a hotch-potch of films of such varied subjects inappropriate in so many ways, but it mattered not; the scenes actually moved. The operator, enclosed in a wooden box with the equipment, revealed no clues as to how it all worked and the audience watched *Dinner Hour at the Factory Gate* or *M. Lumière at Lyons*, *The Landing Stage*, *Small Lifeboat*, *The Arrival of the Paris Express*, *A Practical Joke on the Governess*, *The Fall of a Wall*, and *Bathing in the Mediterranean* to mention a few.

NEXT WEEK!!
AT
THE EMPIRE.

Once Again at Great Expense,

THE ORIGINAL . .
. . UNSURPASSED . .
. . UNEQUALLED

. LUMIERE .

CINEMATOGRAPHE

From the Empire, London,
Under the Direction of M. TREWEY.

A Series of Brilliant and Interesting Scenes absolutely true to life in
PRECISION, PROPORTION AND MOTION.

Towerskay in Moscow.

Children—Cat and Dog.

The Disappointed Artist.

Burmese Dance at the Crystal Palace.

Hamburg Bridge, Germany.

Soldiers' Parade in Madrid.

Concorde Bridge, Paris.

Lancers in Stuttgart.

Artillery in Barcelona.

Fire Brigade Call, London.

Charge of Cavalry in France.

AND

A Remarkable Picture—"TOBOGGANING IN SWITZERLAND."

You would have to expend a large amount of money and time to obtain a view of the Scenes of the above Programme in their Geographical situation, but by the aid of this wonderful instrument in conjunction with Motor Photography, they are brought before you exact in form and motion for the money and time a visit to the Empire entails.

Tudor Printing Works, Cardiff. 14910

1896

Birt Acres filming the 1895 Derby

The Derby in 1895 was filmed by Birt Acres, but it was in 1896 that Robert Paul was commissioned by the Alhambra Music Hall to film the race and have it ready for showing the same evening. Robert Paul on a wagonette with his camera, other equipment and two assistants arrived at Epsom Downs at eight in the morning, taking up a strategic position just past the winning post. The whole set-up attracted much attention and as the winner, Persimmon (owned by the Prince of Wales) thundered past the winning post the camera recorded the event in movement. After the race Mr Paul gathered up the film and returned to London. There he worked far into the night and the film was ready for showing at the Alhambra the following evening. The audience acclaimed the enterprise—the film ran for two and a half minutes—not only because of the topicality and the novelty, but because Persimmon, with its distinguished owner, was such a popular win.

Motion pictures of events taking place opened up limitless possibilities. The Boer War presented an excellent opportunity, but although the camera is said never to lie, the most appalling deceptions were practised on an unsuspecting audience. Pictures said to show a massive charge under battle conditions were, in reality, taken of French cavalry on manoeuvres near Cape Town. When the film was shown at the Pavilion, Tivoli and elsewhere the audience was most enthusiastic and unsuspecting.

The Cyclorama, or Exhibition of Moveable Paintings, and Music Hall in Albany Street, London, 1849. '. . . honoured as the present proprietors have been by the prescence of Her Most Gracious Majesty, His Royal Highness Prince Albert, with other members of the Royal Family, the nobility and *elite* of this country, and many distinguished foreigners, together with the flattering ecomiums bestowed on their efforts by every branch of the Public Press, induce them to believe that the production of works of such unprecedented magnitude and excellence, is fully appreciated by the public as well as by all lovers of Fine Arts.'

Deceptions were exposed in the newspapers, but the novelty of the moving picture remained even if the public ceased to believe what they saw. Films such as *The Embarkation of the Scots Guards* and *Cronje's Surrender to Lord Roberts* were genuine enough, as were any films sponsored by the reputable Mr Paul. He organised a series entitled *Reproductions of Incidents of the Boer War*, the film being 'arranged under the supervision of an experienced military officer from the front'. The series may not have been the real thing, but then it never claimed to be.

Films merely for entertainment were also made and every trick of the trade was employed in the making of them. Tricks like divers emerging from the water feet first, and ghosts appearing in all their transparent glory, stimulated the novel appeal for an increasing audience.

It was after the Queen's death that cinema halls built for the showing of films were established. Even in 1902 when the Alhambra introduced a two-hour programme of films entitled 'Urbanora' it was confined to the afternoon. The gallery was closed, smoking was forbidden in the auditorium, and the audience that assembled to see films of specialised interest was very different from the down-to-earth music hall crowd who clapped and cheered (and booed) in the evening when flesh and blood dominated the stage. Chaplin, Pickford, Lloyd, Fairbanks—they were the names of the future. The tentative beginnings of the film industry at the end of the nineteenth century were the symptoms of a trend that contributed to the death of the music hall and revolutionised entertainment habits.

Meanwhile in many Victorian homes the toy diorama—measuring about 6 x 7½ in—could be enjoyed in comfort. The pictorial strip was gradually unrolled from a cylindrical box and viewed through a cardboard strip.

Simple and great fun were the Thaumatrope discs. On one side of the disc was a riddle with a picture; on the reverse side another picture and an answer to the riddle. Attached to each disc were two lengths of string, and by spinning the disc round, the picture on each side of the disc appeared to merge giving a pictorial answer to the riddle.

There were other equally enjoyable optical devices introducing three-dimensional pictures. Hand-shadows required imagination—and just two hands. By manipulating the fingers animals, birds, human figures and creatures weird and wonderful could be silhouetted against a bare wall, the shadow cast by candlelight or a flickering fire. This could be a very personal entertainment—a do-it-yourself-job played when dusk fell and the curtains were drawn.

Thaumatrope discs. One side the riddle; spin the disc and the answer is revealed!

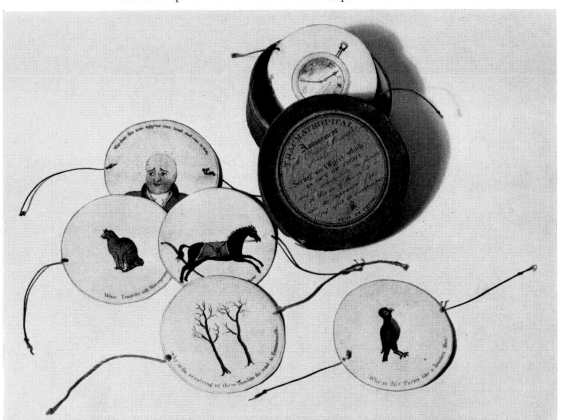

F.

Holidays

Britain, once almost wholly an agricultural country, was becoming industrialised. People flocked to the towns from the country to seek work and wealth. The deplorable conditions under which most of them lived made it essential that they should escape for a time from the smoke and grit that fouled the air they breathed.

The attitude of the employers was unenthusiastic. Leisure was not for the working classes—they did not know how to use it. Besides, the religious days and local fairs were traditional holidays. When trade was slack there was often an enforced 'holiday', but no pay to go with it. Absenteeism became a problem; in certain industries workers stayed away the Monday after pay day, and production was seriously affected.

The Factory Act of 1833 stated that those under eighteen years of age should be 'entitled' to eight half days each year as well as Christmas Day and Good Friday, but the word 'entitled' was used by unscrupulous employers as an excuse not to comply with the Act. The Bank Holiday Act of 1871 and subsequent legislation gave England six Bank Holidays and Scotland five. Holidays with pay were usual in the 1880s and many workers were given Saturday afternoon off.

Ilfracombe, 1894

The pleasure steamer, Jersey, c 1890

First, then, the time for holidays had to be found. Secondly the means of transport to reach the resorts and countryside. Before 1830 travel was a pastime for the wealthy who, if they did not possess a coach, hired one. For others there was the public coach, unreliable and unpunctual. The driver and the inn-keeper were often in league which resulted in the passengers being hurried over their meals and made to pay excessively for food that was indifferent and service that scarcely existed. A coach with four horses travelled at 10 miles an hour, so for a short holiday no very great distance could be covered.

Boys in the sixth form at Dr Arnold's Rugby had never seen the sea and this also applied to much of the population who lacked the time and the means to get there.

The steamers enabled the masses to travel cheaply. Britain's rivers and the sea were used advantageously. The Thames steamer chugged to Gravesend or Margate in six or nine hours depending on the tide. The fare to Gravesend from London was sixpence. Other resorts were becoming increasingly popular. Folkestone might be dull, but it was dignified. For those who wanted a bit of fun there were Yarmouth, Hastings and Southend. Brighton was fashionable, and so were Eastbourne, Bognor and Cowes. Holidaymakers in Yorkshire went to Scarborough and Blackpool. Those living in the Midlands favoured Tenby and Aberystwyth. From Liverpool, boats sailed to the Isle of Man, North Wales and to resorts in Lancashire and Cheshire.

The coming of the railways increased people's mobility, but the steamer remained the cheaper form of transport. The primary object of building railways was to serve industry. As a Select Committee on Railways in 1840 observed, railways were built 'to convey the labourer cheaply and rapidly to that spot where his labour might be most highly remunerated'. In addition, 'the health and enjoyment of the mechanics, artisans, and poor inhabitants of the large towns would be promoted, by the facility with which they would be enabled to remove themselves and their families into healthier districts and less crowded habitations'. The suggestion that people should travel by train for relaxation and pleasure was not considered.

In any case travel by train was an adventure—and not always pleasant at that. There were accidents on the line, the trains were slow and those doomed to travel third class were very uncomfortable indeed.

It was Sir Rowland Hill, chairman of the Brighton Railway Company in the 1840s, who was said to have introduced the 'excursion' train, a form of travel exploited by Mr Thomas Cook, secretary of the South Midland Temperance Society, during that period. The 'excursion' enabled people to travel cheaply, and it was financially advantageous to take a 'return' ticket, or to travel at certain times during the week, and in parties. Firms' outings, school treats and similar occasions enabled considerable fare reductions to be made. Travel by train was a novelty. The stations were crowded with people desperate to get away from the dirt and smoke of the towns into the fresh country air and the

Yarmouth Sands, 1892

Always something happening at the seaside. Yarmouth, c 1890

bracing breezes. People were not particular where they went as long as they were together. An 'excursion' could be a jolly, boisterous occasion with much waving of flags and streamers, and the boom-boom-boom of a bold brass band at the station to speed the party on its way.

The seaside resort, frequented in the coaching days by the dignified aristocracy, found itself invaded by the masses. Accommodation had to be found for all those pouring into the resorts. Builders—many unscrupulous—erected apartment houses, hotels, marine terraces, sea villas, so that original sea views were obliterated by bricks and mortar and many pleasant seaside places became as crowded as the towns. Only the air was purer.

In an 1885 issue of *Punch* there is a picture of a disappointed bank clerk 'enjoying' a Bank Holiday —at home. The verse underneath, dedicated to Sir John Lubbock who was instrumental in bringing in the Bank Holiday Act of 1871, laments:

> The Country crammed—the Seaside jammed—
> The Trains a crush—the River a rush—
> Oh, is it not a jolly day?
> All Shops shut—the Streets all smut—
> No room in the Park for the poor Bank Clerk!
> Not a Bank, but a Blank Holiday.

'Bathing strengthens the interlect, braces the body, clears the system, puts new life in the blood, old heads on to young shoulders, fills the pocket, drives away care, cures corns, warts, bunions, Pilgrims' progresses, water on the brain, *new*-ralgia, *old*-ralgia, velocipedes, bicycles, telephones, tella-crams, and all the Primrose 'ills as flesh is heir to . . .'—Music Hall patter. Yarmouth, 1892

Trippers, Yarmouth, c 1890

The magnet was the sea. The beaches became a mass of humanity; on the promenade a stream of people moved slowly, taking their time, observing all that was going on. Thackeray, seeing Brighton in 1847, noted 'the cabs, the flys, the shandry-dans, the sedan-chairs with the poor invalids inside; the old maids, the dowagers' chariots, out of which you see countenances scarcely less deathlike. . . . The hacks mounted by young ladies from the equestrian schools, by whose side the riding-masters canter confidentially. . . .'

The accommodation the holidaymakers returned to after a bracing day by the sea was in many instances depressing. During the height of the holiday season a bed slept as many as could be uncomfortably crowded into it—perhaps half-a-dozen. There was little comfort and the food was poor. 'Joints, joints, sometimes perhaps, a meat pie, which weighs upon your conscience, with the idea that you have eaten the scraps of other people's dinner,' observed Nathaniel Hawthorne in 1855. Visitors felt—and rightly—they were being fleeced. Many preferred the furnished apartment where they bought their own food and had it cooked for them by the landlady.

But to be awakened in the morning—even if you could not move in bed—by the shrill cries of the seagulls, and to look out of the window at a clear blue sky and perhaps, with luck, get a glimpse of a clear blue sea—that was worth much of the discomfort. Only too soon the work-a-day routine must be resumed.

The difficulty about bathing was the time it took. Impulsively to run into the sea was an impossibility. Paddling was permitted provided only one's feet could be observed. The bathing machine—until the latter part of the century—was a large wooden structure on wheels which had to be hauled by horses to the water's edge according to the tides. On leaving a bathing machine a lady, so covered with voluminous attire that only an ankle protruded, lowered herself into the sea. The costume was indeed forbidding. For the first eighty years of the century heavy pantaloons topped by braid-trimmed dresses were worn. In the eighties a one-piece costume was permitted covering the body from the neck to the knees. Corsets were not discarded before entering the water.

There were strict regulations against 'mixed' bathing. A distance of at least a hundred yards separated the ladies' bathing machines from those of the gentlemen. At Southport a fine of 5 shillings was imposed on any pleasure boat that sailed within thirty yards of where the ladies bathed. A wealthy gentleman with sufficiently good eyesight might be prepared to pay up and possibly did, although what he saw must have been, by present-day standards, bitterly disappointing.

Men frequently bathed naked which was sufficient reason for the distance between the two sexes, and there were complaints that the absence of a 'modesty hood' over the steps of the bathing machine enabled the gentlemen to be seen as they entered the sea. Bathing on Sunday was discouraged. Certain ladies at Brighton armed with prayer books and camp stools, sat on the beach and successfully prevented the gentlemen in the sea from re-entering the bathing machines.

Piers, originally built so that visitors could embark and disembark from steamers, became centres for entertainment. The Margate Pier (rebuilt in 1808 at a cost of £100,000) boasted a gallery in the

1872

LIFE WOULD BE PLEASANT, BUT FOR ITS "PLEASURES."—*Sir Cornewall Lewis*.

In consequence of the English Watering-Places being crowded, People are glad to find Sleeping Accommodation in the Bathing-Machines.

Boots (from Jones's Hotel). "I've brought your Shaving Water, Sir; and you'll please to take care of your Boots on the Steps, Gents: the Tide's just a comin' in!"

OUT OF TOWN.
(UNFASHIONABLE INTELLIGENCE.)
Visitor. "WHAT A ROARING TRADE THE HOTELS WILL BE DOING, WITH ALL THESE HOLIDAY FOLK!"
Head Waiter at The George. "LOR BLESS YER, SIR, NO! THEY ALL BRING THEIR NOSEBAGS WITH 'EM!"

1888

centre where, weather permitting, the band played. In 1812 the penny admission to the pier was hotly resented by a crowd which breached the barrier at the entrance and nearly threw an unfortunate official into the sea. By 1856 Margate had two piers and by 1866 Brighton had added a second pier to the one built in 1823 for the purpose of accommodating Channel steamers.

The high musical standards of the eighteenth century gave way to the blatant brass bands (the players sometimes lubricated with beer from holidaymakers to keep going) of the nineteenth. German bands were exceedingly popular—and not only at seaside resorts—so the visitor was regaled with music wherever he went. Itinerant musicians of doubtful quality had their pitches, and for visitors with more delicate ears, the noise was distasteful. Dickens complained about Broadstairs, Thackeray found the bold brass bands at Dover too much for him, while Mrs Carlyle was appalled at the continuous noise which began at breakfast. While one band rested, its place was taken by Ethiopian musicians or by 'a band of female fiddlers' with a makeweight of 'individual barrel-organs, individual Scotch bagpipes, individual French horns!'

Added to the noise of the brass bands were the fairs and circuses which visited the resorts at high season. Firework displays were popular and the balloon ascents drew big crowds. Sporting activities were confined to fishing and boating, lawn tennis and cricket (neither of these two games was much played until the seventies) and various athletic events in which all could take part.

Riding was a social occupation rather than a sport, and not many swung a golf club with expertise outside Scotland. The quiet, dignified activities such as bowls, archery and croquet flourished until later in the century when life became more energetic.

On the sands the donkeys ambled slowly, the nigger minstrels twanged the familiar melodies, the concert parties, often dressed as pierrots, enchanted holidaymakers of all ages. At the water's edge the quiet shrimping, the collecting of shells, pebbles and varieties of seaweed continued. The taste of shrimps caught in one's own net could not be surpassed, and all the shells, pebbles and seaweed so diligently collected were brought home and lovingly arranged, labelled and admired—a constant reminder of a happy holiday.

The seaside holiday resort with its noise and brashness was fun. And quietly amongst the dunes and rocks it was possible to shut out all the noise and exist in one's own little world. Holidays were hard to come by, so every minute must be enjoyed. Romance might be just round the corner, but the lone male visitor to Jersey in 1887 was duly warned:

> But gentlemen, beware
> And take the greatest care
> Before you lose your heart;
> When you're thinking you have come
> To a charming little plum,
> You may find you have only found a *tart*.

Away from the crowds at Appledore, c 1890

ON THE SANDS!

WRITTEN BY
J. CAULFIELD,

SUNG, WITH IMMENSE SUCCESS, AT
'THE OXFORD,'
BY
W. RANDALL.

London : THE MUSIC-PUBLISHING COMPANY, 19 Peter's Hill, St. Paul's, E.C.
203-4 MUSICAL TREASURY.

The weather was hot and trade was slow,
So to Margate I solv'd to go,
On the Sands, on the Sands, on the Sands, on the Sands.
In a light tweed suit that fitted me well
I went for a week a first rate swell,
On the Sands etc.

Play and Pantomime

The Victorian theatre had much to compete with. The pleasure gardens, taverns, dioramas, circuses all claimed the attention of those seeking entertainment. The somewhat rough behaviour that was evident in certain places of amusement could be seen also in the theatre. In the 1840s the behaviour of some members of the audience was quite disgraceful. Charles Dickens remembers an occasion in 1844 at Sadlers Wells where the audience was 'ruffianly'. He continued, 'It was a bear-garden, resounding with foul language, oaths, cat-calls, shrieks, yells, blasphemy, obscenity. . . . Fights took place anywhere at any period of the performance.' The presence of loose women at the theatre was also deplored. Anyone prepared to accept the risk of becoming involved in a free-for-all, would hesitate before experiencing the discomfort of the seating, the appalling ventilation and the unpleasant smell of oranges. No wonder high society and the middle classes kept well away, the former flocking to the opera where the latest Italian prima donna could fill the house at the drop of an octave; the latter remained at home indulging in the calm domestic pastimes available, or reading suitable books borrowed from Mr Mudie's library.

The standard of acting in the theatre was poor, the emphasis being placed on a good loud voice with little other talent to support it. This form of acting favoured melodrama. Shakespeare was

A protest against the music hall vulgarity of the pantomime, 1883

THE PANTOMIME OF THE FUTURE.—A WARNING.

MUSIC HALL PROFANITY

CHILDREN NOT ADMITTED

TO PANTOMIME IN 1883.

Air—*Refrain of " Caroline! Caroline!" from the Music-Hall Repertoire, of course.*

PANTOMIME! PANTOMIME! THOUGH YOU'VE FAYS THE TRIMMEST,
PANTOMIME! PANTOMIME! YET YOUR FUN'S THE DIMMEST.
OVERDONE WITH SLANG AND CHAFF,
NOTHING TO MAKE THE CHILDREN LAUGH,
WHERE'S YOUR CLEVER, FUNNY PANTOMIMIST?
[*Chorus taken up heartily by old and young Children.*

THE PANTOMIMES

DRURY LANE

HAYMARKET

LYCEUM

ADELPHI

1845

Christmas, 1879

BRITANNIA  THEATRE,

HOXTON,

Stage Boxes, 1s. 6d. Boxes, 1s. Slips and Pit, 6d.

No person admitted to the Boxes unless suitably attired. Omnibusses from all parts of London stop within Two Minutes Walk of the Britannia every Quarter of an hour. Children under Seven Years of Age, Half-Price to Boxes and Pit.

Gallery, equal to the Boxes at any other Theatre, 4d. Back Pit, 3d.

Half-Price at Half-past Eight, to Boxes and Pit. Private Entrance, open at a Quarter-past Five, no extra charge to the Boxes. Performances to commence at half-past Six.

Celeste Stephan — every Evening !

On Monday, January 29th, 1855, and all the Week, will be presented
The Gorgeous Glittering Pantomime, entitled

EGYPT !
3000 Years Ago

A Dream in the

CRYSTAL PALACE.

The Extensive and Gorgeous Scenery of the Opening by
MR. JOHN GRAY.

THE OPENING Written by Mr. W. ROGERS. The COMIC SCENES written by Mr. W. CUSHNIE, and Painted by Mr. C. BULLER.

King Cambyses....Guardian of the Princess—a model for most Kings, a little too fat perhaps, & certainly too good for this vile world..Mr. W. ROGERS, afterwards **Clown** .... **Mons LOUIS**
Prince Rhadamanthus ...his Son—a fast young Man, in love with Polyanthus, who having no idea of bridling his appetites, ought to be sent to BRIDEWELL, afterwards **Harlequin**..MR. W. SMITH
Old Nick, or Nicholas....the Incarnation of Evil, who like a certain Emperor, his namesake, scruples not to set half the world by the ears, Mr. C. PITT, afterwards **Pantaloon** Mr. W. H. NEWHAM
Mandou....a powerful Magician—supposed to be wandering about the Crystal Palace at midnight, no man living having ever seen him there by day .... Mr. C. WILLIAMS
Amos Shortweight................Mr. J. CLEMENTS   Ephraim Grindcorn ......Mr. SACKFILL
Zekiel Clover ... a Farmer, who would not for the world keep up the price of corn ... Mr. Mangel Worzel
The Four Statues....Guardians of the Tomb of Abou Simbel—somewhat tired of sitting 3000 years, and speculating on a rise .... Messrs. Dean, Lucas, Clarke, and Hawkins

The Princess Polyanthus (a Dulcet Warbler) **Miss CLARA ST. CASSE**
Whose notes "—— Come o'er the ear like the sweet South—that breathes upon a bank of Violets—Stealing & giving odours." And who, in the course of the Pantomime, will sing a New Song Written expressly for her :—The Popular Canzonet, called "THE LADIES' NO!" and the Comic Ballad of "THE GIRL WITHOUT A BEAU," afterwards **Harlequina**....................**Miss C. BORROW**
MRS. S. LANE....afterwards Queen Cleopatra, a lady who—(but who does not know Mrs. S. Lane) a Manageress, seeking Materials for a Christmas Pantomime, in the Crystal Palace, with Parodies on the Popular Airs of " Bid the ruddy nectar flow," " Stop that knocking," " The rose shall cease to blow," " Far at sea," " Red, white, & blue," & an air from "Puritani"....**MRS. S. LANE**
Rhelope. . . an Egyptian Lady, who would dance all night, if she might, " By the bright moonlight."
Miss Green, afterwards **Columbine**...... Mdlle. **CELESTE STEPHAN**

Sc. 1. Model of the Tomb of Abou Simbel in the Crystal Palace
Sc. 2. Egypt (as it used to was 3000 years ago) Pavilion of Queen Cleopatra !
IN THE GARDEN OF CEDARS, & DISTANT VIEW OF THE CITY OF PALACES, (by Sunrise)
Scene 3.   Great Pyramid of King Cheops !
Allegorical Representation of the Triple Alliance—ENGLAND, FRANCE, & TURKEY.
SCENE 4.   THE NILE & ENTRANCE TO THE PORT OF PHARAOH RAMESES
Sc. 5. Pyramids of Gizeh & Pilgrims Encamped in the distance
SCENE 6.   MYSTIC APARTMENT IN THE GREAT PYRAMID,
Sc. 7.   Illuminated Point Lace Grotto !
GRAND METEMPSYCHOSIAN TRANSFORMATION
Clown..Mons LOUIS   Pantaloon..Mr W.H.NEWHAM
Harlequin ....   Mr. W. SMITH
Sprites   ....   Messrs. TALLIEN, BROTHERS,
Harlequina..Miss C. BORROW Columbine..Mlle. Celeste STEPHAN
Sc 8-Stunningrog's Gin Palace & Smallcomb's a Wig-maker
TRIP..PAS DE TROIS D' AGREEMENT..HARLEQUIN, COLUMBINE & HARLEQUINA..The jolly fat Boniface of 1851..PANT.." my first is appropriate ; my second is nine to one if you guess it; and my whole overmatches the sole above the earth," what's that! CLOWN.." Why a Parlor."
Sc. 9-BATHS AND WASHHOUSES for the MILLION
TRIP..LA POLKA..HARLEQUIN, COLUMBINE, & HARLEQUINA..PANT. takes a warm bath, and CLOWN does his week's washing..The Rooshuns are coming.." Korniloff and Nacltimoff both off, who'll be next off ! let us hope Romanoff."

FORTRESS OF SEBASTOPOL

Sc. 10-Chickenheart's the Poulterer and Chokemcheap's Manufactory !
TRIP..LA TARANTELLE..HARLEQUIN AND COLUMBINE..PANT..My first is always, m second's durable, and my
Sc. 11---**FURNISHED APARTMENTS**
TRIP..THE UNITY PAS DE TROIS..HARLEQUIN, COLUMBINE, AND HARLEQUINA
Scene 12.   Caius's Juvenile Stage Repository !
AND ROYAL PENNY GAFF !
TRIP-Pas de Trois de Genre—Harlequin, Columbine & Harlequina
Walk up here, walk up, my little dears, No advance in the Prices, only a penny !
SCENE 13.   THE PYRAMID OF BRITANNIA PANTOMIME !!
LAST SCENE.   MR. J. GRAY'S GRAND PANTOMIME ANNUAL.
Interior of the Temple of Memnon in the Land of Egypt ! Brilliant Transformation—
Britannia Presents to her Children,

THE CHRISTMAS TREE !
Illuminated by 1000 Christmas Candles.
Opening of the Shells of the Ocean,   Mystic Growth of the Tree.

After which, every Evening,

MR. HENRY SMITH,
Will give a portion of his celebrated

Vocal Entertainment

Introducing a Selection of those Dramatic, Descriptive and Comic Ballads, in rendering of which, he stands unrivalled.

To conclude with an entirely New, Interesting, Instructive and Didactic Drama, adapted from an admired Tale which recently appeared in " Reynolds's Miscellany," " Family Herald," and " London Journal," and Licensed expressly for this Establishment, to be entitled

Fashion and Famine !

William Leicester..Mr. W. R. Crauford   Robert Olis..Mr. Dean   Benjamin Wilcox..Mr. J. Reynolds
Nicholas ...Mr. W. Rogers   Magistrate of Police Court..Mr. C. Williams
Jacob Strong ....Mr. C. J. Bird
Mr. Acumen..............Mr. C. Pitt   Mr. Smoothly.............Mr. F. Wilton
Judge of the Criminal Court.......Mr. Bedella   Jailor....Mr. Lucas   Jim......Mr. J. Clements
Mulatto Woman.........Mr. Clarke   Creepigny...............Mr. Hawkins
Julia...............Miss C. Borrow   Ada Leicester............Mrs. E. Yarnold
Maude Wilcox....Miss Richardson   Florence....Miss Green   Widow Gray......Mrs. Atkinson
Widow Leicester...Mrs. Mackney   Lilly Clark...Mrs. B. Ware   Sally....Miss Pettifer
Rosana...Miss Davis   Market People, Constables, Ladies and Gentlemen, &c.

The Lone Mansion and its Mistress !
THE VILLAIN & HIS VICTIM. TABLEAU OF EXCITEMENT.
The Old Homestead & Home Memories.
THE STRIDES OF DESTINY. The Last Link Broken. Death of the Betrayed One. EXAMINATION BEFORE THE MAGISTRATES
HALL OF JUSTICE. THE CONDEMNED CELL
The Prisoner under Sentence. The Last Hour—
DEATH OF THE AGED VICTIM

Harlequinade, Adelphi pantomime, 1877

rarely performed—there was no money to be made out of him—until two actor-managers, Samuel Phelps and Charles Kean accomplished the impossible by staging *A Midsummer Night's Dream* at Sadler's Wells.

At first the actors had to leave the stage and eject the more riotous members of the audience. Then, instead of shouting above the noise, they hushed the audience into a more docile mood. Eventually, the working class audience which had caused Dickens so much distress in 1844 was, nearly ten years later, 'a happy crowd, as orderly and reverent as if they were in church, and yet as unrestrained in their enjoyment as if listening to stories told them by their own friends', an observer noted.

People visited the theatre to be taken out of themselves. For many life was drab and sad, so plays full of action were enjoyed. The more blood-thirsty, lustful and passionate the better; the more realistic the scenery and effects the better. A blazing house that was seen to be ablaze was the reality sought after; a well-staged court scene with all the authentic legal trappings was irresistible.

The vast population of London, increased by the network of railways that was beginning to cover the country, consisted of unsophisticated souls eager to absorb what London had to offer, but without the intellectual ability to appreciate good theatre. It was not until the 1860s that new theatres opened and old ones were renovated. Theatregoing was not so uncomfortable; people were no longer herded together like cattle and squeezed into every available space. The new gas lighting was not so stifling

Squire Bancroft and his wife Marie Wilton in *Society*, c 1865

in the hot weather. Audiences behaved better although the sucking of oranges continued to be a disturbing distraction and the smell of them even more so.

Comedy became popular, and a play, *Society*, which opened in November 1865 ran for 150 performances and the handsome young actor in it, Mr Bancroft, became the topic of conversation in the drawing rooms of Mayfair. T. W. Robertson, the play's author and of numerous other amusing comedies of that period, created a suitable climate to bring people back into the theatre. 'The Teacup and Saucer' drama as it was called, made the theatre fashionable and those who had filled the opera house now filled the stalls of the theatres.

The seventies saw the arrival of numerous theatrical managements whose object was financial gain rather than a desire to improve dramatic quality. Others of noble birth, weary of waiting at the stage door, could, by being financially involved in the production of a play, ensure that a part was written for his lady of the moment. It made access to her so much simpler. Irving's appearance as Hamlet in 1874 was the event of the decade. His production and portrayal of the part heralded a new interpre-

A DISENCHANTMENT.

Very Unsophisticated Old Lady (from the extremely remote country). "DEAR ME! HE'S A VERY DIFFERENT-LOOKING PERSON FROM WHAT I HAD ALWAYS IMAGINED!"

'To be, or not to be : that is the question . . .'. Act III, Scene I

tation of Shakespeare. Gilbert and Sullivan, after an unsuccessful production of *Thespis, or The Gods Grown Old* at the Gaiety in 1871 tried again under the management of D'Oyly Carte in 1875 at the Royalty with the popular and much acclaimed *Trial by Jury*.

In the eighties some audiences accepted what they saw on the stage as real life and were incapable of applying their limited intelligence to serious drama. Others found amusement in plays that were of serious intent, but an educated public was emerging eager for plays that endeavoured to interpret life as it was lived rather than how it was supposed to be lived.

Managers, or more often actor-managers, attempted to cater for individual audiences who were interested in a particular form of drama. Burlesque could be seen at the Gaiety; farce flourished at the Strand and Vaudeville; melodrama was played at the Adelphi and Surrey; Shakespeare and romantic drama could be seen at the Lyceum; comedy at the Haymarket.

By the turn of the century the theatre was accepted socially. The white ties and tails, the sables and jewellery adorned the stalls. The uncouth in the pit—often the most worthwhile seats in the house for the price—were the true experts who understood drama and gave vociferous indications of their approval or disapproval about what was performed on stage. So vocal did they become that the Bancrofts abolished the pit at the Haymarket in 1880. This resulted in violent demonstrations by the pit habitués and six years later the cheated 'pittites' were still demonstrating outside the Haymarket Theatre.

The Victorian dramatists—Pinero, Arthur Jones, R. C. Carton, Boucicault, Barrie and Shaw in their early days, and Oscar Wilde, set the scene. Irving, Terry, Benson and Tree were some of the great performers who gave the theatre the purpose that was lacking at the beginning of the Queen's reign.

In 1880 *The Times* lamented, 'save for its two strongholds in Drury Lane and Covent Garden, which still defy the assaults of fashion and the sap of change, Pantomimes may now be considered as wholly relegated to the suburbs of London'.

The decline of pantomime dated from Mr Grimaldi's farewell night at Sadler's Wells on 17 March 1828. With his retirement the tradition of the Clown, Harlequin, Pantaloon and Columbine along with other Harlequinade characters, withered. There was nobody to match Grimaldi and by 1867 it was lamented that *The Forty Thieves* at Covent Garden was 'all legs and limelight'. There was a tendency for the chief parts in a pantomime to be taken by music hall artistes, instead of by actors and actresses from the 'legitimate' stage, and *The Times* commented on 'the corruption of Boxing Day morals through the influence of the music hall'.

Away from the bright lights of Covent Garden and Drury Lane the Britannia—known as the 'Old Brit'—in Hoxton staged a pantomime that drew full houses night after night. The theatre, situated in a dismal back street, was difficult to find and difficult to reach, but for five solid hours without an interval the pantomime was played, the audience sustaining themselves with sandwiches. A recitation by the Fairy Queen was a signal to make a rush for the bar and drink as much liquid as possible by the time the recitation had ended. With clever timing one could be back in the auditorium when the knock-about, comic scenes and popular songs were taking place. The 'Old Brit' was possibly the last theatre to retain the genuine old fashioned Harlequinade. Two other theatres where traditional panto-mime could be seen were the Pavilion, Mile End (known affectionately as 'the Drury Lane of the East') and the old Standard Theatre in Shoreditch.

But the magic remained. The excitement of the dark theatre, then suddenly the footlights on, the red glow at the bottom of the heavy curtain and now, slowly, slowly the curtain rising transporting young and old alike into a new world.

Walk Up! Walk Up!

The colourful travelling circus received a welcome wherever it went. Alongside the lumbering, gaily painted vehicles the excited children ran shouting and laughing in anticipation of the wonders that would be revealed when the Big Top was erected on the village green. It was for many living in remote districts the only entertainment of the year.

Wild's and Bannister's were familiar to the inhabitants of the northern and midland counties. Saunders's, Cooke's, Samwell's and Clarke's toured the eastern, southern and western areas. Many of the tenting circuses were on a modest scale and could be seen mainly at fairs. There were seldom more than three or four horses and the entire 'cast' would assemble outside the tent to attract an audience. The acrobats did some handsprings and 'flips, and the clown wisecracked while the proprietor banged a gong or drum, shouting at the hesitant spectators to 'walk up, walk up'. The horses stood patiently in a row on the platform.

When the house was full the proprietor would give the drum a final bang and shout, 'All in, to

The circus comes to Alton in Hampshire, 1899

Fair near Battersea Park, c 1890

begin' and the horses, acrobats and clown would enter the tent and the show would open. The performances were short, consisting of two or three acts of horsemanship, some acrobatics, and tight-rope walking, but from noon to midnight they worked as often as there were people willing to fill the seats. And after each performance the company would assemble outside the tent to entice the newcomers. It was a hard life.

'Lord' George Sanger established his circus by buying a Welsh pony and a horse. The pony was trained to do unusual tricks such as card-picking and fortune telling, and the horse was trained to gallop in circus fashion round the yard at a public house. In the summer he acquired a clown and other artistes and opened at the Chester Fair in King's Lynn. He travelled the eastern counties with such success that he was soon able to enlarge the circus. After doing well at Manchester he was able to buy nine more horses and two ponies. A popular tour of Scotland enabled him to raise the prices of admission from a penny and threepence to sixpence, a shilling and even two shillings.

The more permanent circus was established in Great Britain towards the end of the eighteenth century by Philip Astley and due to his efforts the circus increased in popularity during the Victorian era. Astley was a cavalry sergeant and when he was discharged from the army he married the daughter of a trick rider. In a field on the site of the present Waterloo Station he erected a roped-in ring and with two horses (one of which had been presented to him when he left the army) gave an equestrian display to whoever cared to stop and watch. At the end of each performance he went round with the hat and the audience dropped into it the odd halfpenny. This impromptu circus was well received so

Astley's next venture was to build a crude circus on a piece of ground near Westminster Bridge. The ring was in the open air but the spectators were under cover and it was known as the Amphitheatre. Astley died in 1814 and his son, who had taken over on his father's death, died a few years later.

Philip Astley bought his horses at Smithfield and rarely paid more than a fiver for one. He was the best trainer of his day and it is claimed he was the first to teach horses to 'dance' in time to the music.

In 1830 Astley's was managed by Andrew Ducrow whose equestrian acts were internationally famous. 'Astley's' became a name that implied the best in the public's mind. When the season was over there was a demand for equestrian acts at Drury Lane and Covent Garden productions and it was 'Astley's' who supplied them. As Dickens wrote of it, 'Dear, dear, what a place it looked that Astley's; with all the paint, gilding and looking glass; the vague smell of horses suggestive of coming wonders; the curtain that hid such gorgeous mysteries; the clean white sawdust in the circus; the company coming in and taking their places; the fiddlers looking carelessly up at them while they tuned their instruments. . . . What a glow was that, which burst upon them all; when the long, clear, brilliant row of lights came slowly up. . . .' That was the overture that delighted the Victorians and their children when more sophisticated forms of entertainment were not available to them.

Interior of 'Astleys' Amphitheatre—the colour scheme was white, lemon, green and gold, with rich crimson hangings from the private boxes, 1843

Astley's Amphitheatre in 1854. A terrific spectacle doubtless slightly exaggerated by the artist, but one hopes not.

The Great Exhibition

The wonders of the 1851 Exhibition are well known, but even before it opened, the building of the Crystal Palace in Hyde Park was one of the sights of London. Spectators hindered the workmen who were working on a tight schedule, and the contractors charged 5s a head for a close view of what was going on. Even this sum did not prevent about two hundred people daily paying in order that they might wander and wonder.

On the opening day, Thursday 1 May, there were upwards of half a million people in the park. Small boys swarmed up trees for the best view, and there was a danger that Rotten Row would lose its dignity if it was not kept clear of people. The park was a camping ground for thousands who danced and slept on the grass. The Duke of Wellington invited a number of small children to watch the scene from Apsley House, and all roads leading to the park were packed with vehicles scarcely moving.

Military bands, deployed strategically, ensured that there was music coming from every quarter, and in a secluded corner of the park a balloon was being inflated.

From the beginning the Exhibition was a success. Everything was done to encourage the 'working classes' to visit it. Mr Thomas Harrison of Ranelagh Road, Pimlico accommodated 1,000 persons per night in his Mechanic's Home for 1851, close by Mr Cubitt's Pimlico Pier where steam boats arrived from the City every ten minutes (the fare from London Bridge to the pier was twopence).

The building, erected on the site of a furniture depository destroyed by fire, occupied two acres and possessed two huge sleeping rooms and two smaller dormitories. Every lodger had his own cubicle and the rooms, lit by gas, were supervised by 'warders'. There were dining, reading and smoking rooms, a news room which not only contained the current newspapers and magazines but all publications relating to the Exhibition and the sights of London, free of charge. A band played in the smoking-room, and from the top of the building lodgers could 'obtain an excellent view of the river and the surrounding country'.

A 'very decent breakfast' cost fourpence or sixpence, and a good dinner eightpence. Lodging charges were 1s 3d a night 'including attendance, and soap, towels, and every convenience of ablution'. Boots were cleaned for a penny a pair and the barber attended to the heads and chins of the lodgers for the same price. A doctor was in attendance every morning at nine o'clock. The omnibus service from the Mechanic's Home to the Exhibition ran frequently and the fare was a penny.

When the Exhibition was first opened there was a good chance of seeing the Queen who honoured it with a visit every other day. She would come before the doors opened at 10 o'clock and walk carefully round the building, stopping at the stands and praising when she felt praise was due, or criticising gently when she considered it deserved.

On the day when admission was only a shilling the Exhibition drew crowds of 70,000. Country people arrived in what an observer referred to as 'rustic' dresses, with their children and ample provisions. The railways brought them to London and from the stations they were conveyed by waggon to Hyde Park. A clergyman of a parish would come with his entire flock. Commanding officers sent soldiers and sailors, and hundreds of charity children, conspicuously dressed, went round the halls in single file.

Saturday morning, until mid-day, was set aside for the crippled and infirm who were pushed round the Exhibition in wheel chairs. This concession was occasionally abused when 'cripples', once in the building, threw away their crutches, leaped from their wheel chairs and strolled round the building like the normal visitor who was admitted an hour or so later.

Although many visitors came with provisions there were refreshments on sale in the hall itself. The

SCENE—EXHIBITION REFRESHMENT ROOM.

Visitor. "Pint o' Beer, Miss, Please."

Miss. "Don't keep it. You can have a Strawberry Ice and a Wafer!"

The Exhibition was 'dry'

1851

'I never saw Hyde Park look as it did, being filled with crowds as far as the eye could reach. A little rain fell, just as we started, but before we reached the Park, the sun shone and gleamed upon the gigantic *edifice*, upon which the flags of every nation were flying.'

—from Queen Victoria's diary

tender for the catering went to Messrs Schweppe & Co, The Soda Water Manufacturers, who paid £5,500 for the privilege. Wine, beer and spirits could not be sold, nor could they be admitted, but the refreshing cup of tea was available. Bread and butter, cheese, ices, pastry, sandwiches, patties, fruits, tea, coffee, chocolate, cocoa, lemonade, ginger beer, seltzer and, of course, soda water could be bought, but as no cooking of any kind was permitted in the building visitors had to be content with cold meat and steamed potatoes if they required anything more satisfying.

Such limited catering facilities can hardly have pleased the numerous foreign visitors, and it was a Frenchman who commented that the buffets served 'fearful' pastries and 'horrible creams that would be ices', but it must be remembered that he was a Frenchman and possibly unable to appreciate the attractions of English catering.

It is recorded that during the course of the Exhibition a total of 934,691 Bath buns and 870,027 plain buns and 1,092,337 bottles of non-alcoholic liquid were consumed and presumably digested.

The same Frenchman who had criticised the catering, noticed that the British reserve was no longer so obvious. 'In very truth,' he wrote, 'I think they are becoming social and familiar. They have always been polite and hospitable to those who bring proper introductions to them, but now one actually meets some who enter into conversation without that preliminary condition.'

He might well be right. During the 140 days of the Exhibition three petticoats, two bustles, three pincushions and twelve monocles were abandoned by their owners and never claimed, but nobody died in the building and one baby was born.

108

Page from a Victorian scrapbook

Bibliography

A Description of The Royal Colosseum etc (1849)

Altham, H. S. *A History of Cricket* (1962)

Berlyn, Peter. *A Popular Narrative of the Origin, History, Progress and Prospects of the Great Industrial Exhibition 1851* (1851)

Bunsen, Victoria de. *Old and New in the Countryside* (1920)

Cook, O. *Movement in Two Dimensions* (1963)

Disher, M. Willson. *The Greatest Show on Earth* (1937)

Frost, Thomas. *Circus Life and Circus Celebrities* (1875)

Greville, Lady. *The Gentlewoman in Society* (1892)

Hackwood, Frederick W. *Old English Sports* (1907)

Haddon, Archibald. *The Story of the Music Hall* (1935)

Hayes, L. M. *Reminiscences of Manchester from the Year 1840* (1905)

Hibbert, H. G. *A Playgoer's Memories* (1920)

Hobhouse, Christopher. *1851 and the Crystal Palace* (1950)

Hoffman, Professor. *Drawing-Room Amusements and Evening Party Entertainments* (1879)

Hudson, Lynton. *The English Stage 1850-1950* (1951)

Lardner, Dr, reviewed by. *The Great Exhibition, and London in 1851* (1852)

Low, Rachel and Manvell, Roger. *The History of the British Film 1896-1906* (1948)

Macqueen-Pope, W. *Shirt Fronts and Sables* (1953)

Mander, Raymond and Mitchenson, Joe. *A Picture History of the British Theatre* (1957)

Manning-Sanders, Ruth. *Seaside England* (1951)

Margetson, Stella. *Leisure and Pleasure in the 19th Century* (1969)

McKechnie, Samuel. *Popular Entertainment Through the Ages* (1932)

Oakley, C. A. *Where We Came In* (1964)

Payn, James. *Some Literary Recollections* (1884)

Pelham, Camden. *The Chronicles of Crime; or The New Newgate Calendar* etc (1891)

Perugini, Mark Edward. *Victorian Days and Ways* (1936)

Pimlott, J. A. R. *The Englishman's Holiday: A Social History* (1947)

Pulling, Christopher. *They Were Singing* (1952)

Rowell, George. *The Victorian Theatre: A Survey* (1956)

Russell, J. F. and Elliot, J. H. *The Brass Band Movement* (1936)

Stuart, Charles Douglas and Park, A. J. *The Variety Stage* (1896)

Thomson, J. and Smith, A. *Street Life in London* (1877)

Walbank, F. A. *Queens of the Circulating Library* (1950)

Wroth, Warwick. *Cremorne and the Later London Gardens* (1907)

Wroth, W. and A. E. *The London Pleasure Gardens of the 18th Century* (1896)

Young, G. M. (editor). *Early Victorian England 1830-1865* 2 vols (1934)

Acknowledgements

The books listed on the opposite page were of great assistance and my thanks are due to the authors past and present. The illustrations are from a variety of sources most of which are listed below. I am grateful for the permission granted to reproduce them.

A.D.

Illustrations
Punch: pages 8, 9, 10, 11, 18, 19, 20, 21, 22, 23, 71, 72, 73 (both), 89, 90, 93, 100 (left), 107
The Tate Gallery, London: pages 12, 66
Victoria and Albert Museum (photographs by Paul Martin): pages 26 (lower), 27, 28, 82, 84, 85, 86, 87, 88, 103
Victoria and Albert Museum (Crown Copyright): pages 95, 96, 97, 98, 99, 100 (right), 105
Kensington and Chelsea Public Libraries: pages 29, 30, 31, 35
Illustrated London News: pages 32, 33, 36, 37, 41, 54, 55, 56, 57, 70, 94, 104, 108
Greater London Council: pages 38, 39
Manchester Public Libraries: pages 43, 44
Raymond Manderson and Joe Mitchenson: pages 48, 50, 51, 52, 83, 92
National Army Museum: page 60
Yorkshire Rugby Football Union: page 61 (painting by W. B. Woollen)
William Gordon Davis: pages 62, 63, 68, 69, 74, 75
The Croquet Association, Hurlingham: page 64
National Film Archive: pages 78, 79
Barnes Museum of Cinematography, St Ives, Cornwall: page 81
A Country Camera by Gordon Winter, published by David & Charles: page 102
Mary Evans Picture Library: page 109
Coloured frontispiece and jacket illustration by kind permission of The London Museum

Index

Figures in italic type indicate an illustrated reference